CONTROLLING
WEEDS

Created and designed by
the editorial staff of ORTHO BOOKS

PROJECT EDITOR
Susan A. Roth

WRITER
Barbara H. Emerson

ARTIST
Amy Bartlett Wright

PHOTOGRAPHER
Saxon Holt

PHOTO EDITOR
Pamela Peirce

GRAPHIC DESIGN
Finger Vesik Smith

Ortho Books

Editorial Director
Christine Robertson

Production Director
Ernie S. Tasaki

Managing Editors
Michael D. Smith
Sally W. Smith

System Manager
Katherine L. Parker

National Sales Manager
Charles H. Aydelotte

Marketing Specialist
Dennis M. Castle

Operations Assistant
Georgiann Wright

Administrative Assistant
Francine Lorentz-Olson

Distribution Specialist
Barbara F. Steadham

Senior Technical Analyst
J. A. Crozier, Jr., PhD.

Chevron Chemical Company
6001 Bollinger Canyon Road, San Ramon, CA 94583

Acknowledgments

Copy Chief
Melinda E. Levine

Copyeditor
Susan Lang

Editorial Coordinator
Cass Dempsey

Layout & Pagination by
Linda M. Bouchard

Editorial Assistants
Nicole Barrett
Tamara Mallory

Proofreader
Deborah N. Bruner

Production by
Lezlly Freier

Systems Coordinator
Laurie Steele

Art Director
Craig Bergquist

Indexer
Shirley J. Manley

Color Separations by
Color Tech Corp.

Lithographed in USA by
Webcrafters, Inc.

Consultants
Walter Skroch, PhD.
  Professor Weed Science
  North Carolina State
  University
  Raleigh, N.C.

Kirk Hurto, PhD.
  Lawn Research Scientist
  Columbus, Ohio

The author wishes to thank the following for their helpful advice:
Arthur Bing, PhD.
Clyde Elmore, PhD.
Larry Kuhns, PhD.
Jimmy R. Massey, PhD.
Rupert Palmer, PhD.
Andrew Senesac, PhD.

Special Thanks
Ames Lawn and Garden
  Tools, Parkersburg, W. Va.
Blake Garden, Kensington,
  Calif.
Mrs. Helen Clark
CoClico Gilland Landscape
  Design, San Francisco,
  Calif.
Joseph DesJardins
Emmy Erlich
Gardener's Supply, Burlington, Vt. (Distributors of
  Magic Weeder hand tools)
Insight Landscaping, San
  Francisco, Calif.
Judy Jamerson
David and Lisa Kruse
John Norcross
Norma Pomerance
Stutz-Davis Co., Inc., Los
  Angeles, Calif.
  (Distributors of Solo
  backpack sprayers)
Warren's Turf Professionals,
  Suisun City, Calif. (Makers
  of Warren's Weed Arrest,
  a fabric mulch)

Photographers
William D. Adams: 17T, 31, 48R, 61TL, 63T
Dr. Phillip Banks: 60R
Rosalind Creasy: 35, 41T, 41B, 42
Al Crozier: 18, 25T, 25B
Michael A. Dirr: 73TL, 77R
Clyde Elmore: 48L, 49R, 58L, 62B, 64TL, 82BL, 83L, 84BL, 86R, 87BR, back cover TR
Barbara Emerson: 6, 51C, 54TL, 54B, 60TL, 60BL, 62T, 64TR, 65L, 67R, 69T, 69B, 72TL, 74TL, 75L, 75R, 79R, 81, 82TL, 89R, 91L, 91R, 92L
Kenneth W. Fink (Berg and Associates): 72R
Charles Marden Fitch: Front cover BL, 46, 55TR, 64B, 68L, 79L, 79C, 86L
Saxon Holt: 14, 19, 20T, 20B, 21T, 21B, 22, 23, 26, 28, 30T, 30B, 34T, 34B, 36, 38, 39T, 39B, 43, 45TL 45TR, 45B, back cover TL, BR
Gene Joyner: 58R, 61BL
William M. Lewis, North Carolina State University: 49L, 70R, 76TR, 89L
P. Lindtner: 59B, 73BL, 83R, 85R, 88BR
John A. Lynch: 52B, 54TR, 55BR, 65TR, 74BL, 76BR, 78R, 90T, back cover BL
Pam Peirce: Front cover TL and CL, 7TL, 10, 12TL, 12TC, 12TR, 17B, 56, 66L, 72BL, 73R, 80T, 84R
Susan A. Roth: 4, 7TR, 29
Anita Sabarese: Front cover TR, C, and BR, 52T, 53B, 57R, 58C, 59T, 61R, 63B, 65BR, 65C, 66R, 70L, 74R, 77L, 80B, 84TL, 87TL, 87BL, 88L, 88TR, 90B
John Serrao: 51R, 71C
Kay Shaw: 50R
John J. Smith: Front cover TC, title page, 12B, 50L, 51L, 53T, 55L, 57L, 68R, 71R, 76L, 87TR, 92C
Wardene Weisser (Berg and Associates): 71L, 82R, 85L, 92R
Ron West: 7B, 67L, 67C, 70C, 78L

Front cover
Top left: Close-up of a dandelion flower head shows individual blossoms.
Top center: Chicory has attractive flowers but is a deep-rooted pest in a lawn.
Top right: The waving seed heads of yellow foxtail, an annual weedy grass, disperse numerous seeds.
Center left: These young cabbage plants are about to be buried under a blanket of common chickweed.
Center right: Bullthistle is among the many weeds with sharp spines that threaten the gardener.
Bottom left: Milkweed seeds have silky hairs that carry them off into the breeze.
Bottom right: Red leaves on poison-ivy mark the coming of autumn.

Title page
Some weeds appear graceful and beautiful, but many, such as this Japanese knotweed, will not stay in bounds.

Back cover
Top left: Weeding a flower bed with a hoe.
Top right: Annual bluegrass, a common grassy weed.
Bottom left: Canada thistle, a deep-rooted perennial weed.
Bottom right: Using a hose-end sprayer to apply herbicide to a lawn.

CONTROLLING WEEDS

UNDERSTANDING WEEDS

Besides making a garden look unsightly, weeds rob desirable plants of nutrients, water, and light. Where do weeds come from? How do they spread? How do they reproduce? Here are some answers.

Page 5

USING HERBICIDES SAFELY AND EFFECTIVELY

With lawn and garden weed killers, controlling weeds can be easy, efficient, and effective. Learn the different ways herbicides work and how to apply them correctly.

Page 15

NONCHEMICAL METHODS OF WEED CONTROL

Deep mulching, regular hoeing, and even hand-pulling can help deter weeds. Find out which mulches and types of tools will do the best job.

Page 27

SELECTING THE RIGHT CONTROL METHODS

Controlling weeds in vegetable gardens requires a different plan of attack than does combating them in a lawn. Learn which techniques work best for each garden area.

Page 37

ENCYCLOPEDIA OF WEEDS

Here is a rogues' gallery of common lawn and garden weeds. A mug shot of each weed aids in its identification, and the text describes how to best combat it.

Page 47

UNDERSTANDING WEEDS

Shepherdspurse

All around the world gardeners find their joy shadowed by a common problem: weeds. This has probably been true ever since agriculture began. Although ancient civilizations had uses for most plants, early Sumerians, Egyptians, and Greeks, centuries before the time of Christ, had a name for plants they considered undesirable. The word as we know it today traces back to Anglo-Saxons in the time of King Alfred when August was known as *weod monath*—the month of weeds.

It is reassuring to know that among the many thousands of kinds of plants, only a couple of hundred are undesirable enough to be considered important weeds. Relatively few North American weeds are native to North America. Most have come to this continent from Europe and Asia as stowaway immigrants.

Some weeds, such as wild onion and prickly pear, grow both in the wild and in cultivated places. Others, such as bindweed, wild radish, and ryegrass, have never been found in the wild, and seem to grow only in association with people's activities. Still others, such as Johnsongrass, kudzu, Japanese honeysuckle, multiflora rose, the attractive little slender speedwell, and the bulbous African oxalis that dots California lawns and gardens, were originally brought here for specific purposes, either for animal forage, for erosion control, or as attractive ornamentals. They spread so rapidly that they became serious pests. A trumpet vine (*Campsis radicans*) that attracts hummingbirds is sold in nurseries in the North but is a rampant pest in warmer climates like Texas.

Weeds thwart a gardener's plans and make landscapes look untidy. Dandelions, with their conspicuous yellow flowers, are one of the most common weeds.

Besides making a garden look unsightly, weeds rob desirable plants of nutrients, water, and sunlight. Where do weeds come from? How do they spread? How do they reproduce? Here are some answers.

The calla lily sold as a florist pot plant romps through California gardens. Bittersweet and wisteria, handsome as they are, twining wild in the edges of woodlands can strangle and smother trees.

Just as there are many different kinds of weeds, there are many variations among the problems they present and many ways of resolving these problems. Learning about the ways of weeds and the range of possibilities that can be used to control them is the first step toward eliminating them. The better gardeners understand weeds, the better they will be able to avoid the undesirable effects of weeds.

Part of this understanding comes from finding out about a weed's life cycle—that is, how and when it grows and reproduces. Once you understand what makes the weed a weed, you can decide which methods will work best to control or eradicate it. Control methods include chemical, cultural, and mechanical techniques. Some methods work more effectively on different weeds, depending upon their particular habits, and often it takes a combination of techniques to win the battle. Where the weed is growing—in a lawn, in pathways, or elsewhere—makes a difference too.

As you learn to recognize different weeds and understand the arsenal of controls at your command, you will begin to see how to control or eliminate weeds on your property. You will know how to defeat weeds in a lawn, in flower beds, in vegetable gardens, beneath trees and shrubs, and in open areas surrounding your home.

This book is intended to help you recognize the most common and troublesome weeds, understand their aggressive ways, and know how to best control them. You will find more details about control methods in the following chapters and in the Encyclopedia of Weeds, beginning on page 47.

Although this book primarily addresses the problems that weeds cause, weeds do have some good points too, particularly the ability to penetrate soil deeply. They often help break up heavy soil, and bring mineral nutrients from deeper in the soil up to the surface. Many weeds, such as Queen Anne's lace, possess a beauty of their own—a beauty that's more often appreciated in a natural area and less often in a garden.

WHY CONTROL WEEDS?

Why is it so important to get rid of weeds, anyway? Despite their messy look, the main reason to eliminate weeds is that they are often out-and-out robbers. Most are aggressive plants; that's how they survive in spite of much adversity. Their aggressiveness is often the characteristic that defines them as weeds.

Weeds As Aggressors

It's a competitive world, even among plants, and the fittest are those that survive. Weeds can compete because they often absorb a disproportionate amount of the mineral nutrients and water available in the soil around them. This is most evident when one or more growth factors, such as nitrogen, are in short supply. Because they grow so fast, the weeds gobble up the available soil nutrients and moisture leaving less for the more desirable, slower-growing garden plants.

With such competition it's not surprising when the less aggressive plants you prefer don't grow as well as they would have in a weed-free garden. Their vigor is reduced and so are the amounts and quality of their flowers or fruits. The difference might not be noticeable with only a few weeds present, but becomes more evident as more weeds invade.

Weeds can cause very significant crop reductions: 10 to 50 percent or more depending on the circumstances. This is dramatically demonstrated when compar-ing the growth of large numbers of plants as in a cornfield. Corn plants growing without competition from weeds are taller, more vigorous, and better able to withstand drought and any insect or disease damage than the weedy corn growing right next to them. The weed-free corn yields more and the ears are fuller, too. If the competition is great enough, the weed-choked corn becomes stunted and turns pale green; it wilts sooner during a drought. Its poor yield results mainly from being unable to absorb as much water and mineral nourishment as is needed.

Competition is especially keen between germinating seedlings that you have planted and weed seeds already in the ground. Roots develop many times faster than do the aboveground parts, and they reach out voraciously for nutrients and water. It is surprising to realize that it is these tender little weedlings, rather than the already established weeds, that do the most to suppress the seedlings you're trying to encourage.

Partly because they are so vigorous, weeds also steal light and space by shading lower-growing or less competitive plants. Adequate light is essential to plants because it powers the process of photosynthesis whereby green leaves convert the sun's energy into the sugars and starches essential for plant growth. By competing for space, prostrate weeds like purslane and chickweed can crowd out and physically smother less vigorous plants, either deforming them or killing them outright. They often do this to onion, vining cucumber, lettuce, and other plants whose foliage casts little shade. Crabgrass, ground ivy, chickweed, and many other creeping weeds smother lawn grass in this way. Clambering vines, such as bindweed on the ground or honeysuckle and kudzu twining up shrubs and trees, do much the same thing.

Weeds don't steal space just on land. Aquatic weeds can interfere with boating and swimming enjoyment, especially in the shallow edges of lakes or ponds. Colonies of waterweed tickling your body don't add much fun to swimming. They can also foul the propellers of motorboats and frustrate attempts to fish, besides spoiling the appearance of the water's surface.

The ultimate competition is achieved by parasitic plants, those that get all their nourishment from the tissues of a host plant to which they are attached. Great football-like clumps of mistletoe in shade trees or orange strands of dodder threading their way through a favorite shrub are unsightly as well as damaging; they are almost impossible to control without destroying the host plant.

Weeds compete with desirable plants for water. Unweeded corn (left) shows water stress, though weeded corn (right) does not.

Weeds and Allelopathy

Certain weeds, and even desirable plants, can compete with other plants by a kind of chemical warfare called allelopathy. An allelopathic plant secretes a growth-inhibiting (or sometimes growth-stimulating) substance. This substance is absorbed by another, sensitive species. The growth-altering chemical may be ex-uded from roots into the soil, or it may be leached from the leaves to drip into the soil or onto the plants below. Some gardeners may have seen the toxic effects suffered by tomato, apple, and other plants growing at the base of a black wal-nut tree. The seedlings of green foxtail, a common garden weed, can prevent cab-bage and corn from growing normally. Common ryegrass, a garden weed found in inexpensive seed mixtures, can keep newly sown bluegrass and other desirable turfgrasses from germinating. In addition to their competitive capabilities, quack-grass rhizomes can negatively affect over a hundred different plant species. This inhibitory effect is due to a complex relationship with soil bacteria as the quackgrass roots decay.

Weeds As Insect and Disease Hosts

Most gardeners may not be aware of two other less obvious problems caused by weeds. Natural chemicals in certain plants actually attract specific insects and nematodes (microscopic worms that live in the soil and feed on plants); some har-bor diseases that can spread to desirable plants. For instance, weedy members of the nightshade family, including horsenettle and groundcherry, can harbor insects that attack their garden rel-atives—tomato, pepper, eggplant, and potato. If you've grown potatoes you have most likely seen leaves chewed by the red larvae and striped adults of the Colorado potato beetle. These pests for-age on weedy nightshades but prefer their vegetable garden relatives when these are available. The big, fat sweet po-tato, tobacco, and tomato hornworms have similar habits.

Some weedy mustards are hosts to cabbage loopers, which feed on many garden plants including petunia, gera-nium, tomato, pea, and members of the cabbage family. Common ragweed at-tracts many different insects that can then visit your garden favorites.

This kind of chumminess isn't limited to insects. Certain weeds are alternate hosts for plant diseases. The disease or-ganism spends part of its life cycle on one kind of plant and the other part on an entirely different plant species. Weeds

are sometimes one of the hosts in such a disease cycle; eliminate the weed and you spare the desirable plant. A number of mustard-family weeds and velvetgrass are hosts to the club root disease of cabbage-family crops. Quackgrass and common chickweed host root-rot, which infects many garden plants. Purslane, pig-weed, and other weeds are alternate hosts to *rhizoctonia*, a serious root disease on rhododendron and relatives.

Some plant virus diseases have alter-nate hosts and can be spread from one plant to another by insects. The virus re-mains underground on roots through the winter and is then transmitted by insects to other types of plants the next spring. Horsenettle, one of these alternate hosts, may harbor tomato mosaic virus or any of several important diseases and insect

Top left: These healthy weeds are competing with the onions for water and nutrients now, and, if the weeds aren't pulled, some, such as the round-leaved mal-lows, will soon grow tall enough to compete for sunshine as well.
Top right: Some weeds climb over shrubs and trees, robbing them of light and making landscapes look untidy; here are Japanese honeysuckle (yellow leaves) and English ivy (green leaves).
Bottom: Weeds often harbor pests that can spread to garden plants. Spider mites have covered this wild nightshade with their webbing.

pests incuding the familiar flea beetle that often reduces leaves of eggplant, tomato, and many other plants to lacework. The aster yellows virus has been found in 67 weed species; leafhoppers feeding on the weeds transmit the virus to asters in the garden. Other leafhoppers surviving on shepherdspurse weeds between crop periods transmit a virus that causes curlytop disease in bean and tomato plants.

Weeds As Health Hazards

Pollen and irritating oils from some plants, including weeds and ornamentals, can cause allergic reactions. Most people have encountered the itching red skin and blisters that can result from contact with the toxic resins of poison ivy, poison oak, and poison sumac—or they have suffered from hay fever caused by windbown pollen. Weeds like common or giant ragweed, bermudagrass, and orchardgrass are prime examples. They can cause distressing allergies as hay fever sufferers know only too well. Goldenrod has often been accused of contributing to respiratory troubles, but scientists now believe the pollen is unlikely to cause allergies. Its pollen grains are large and waxy, and not readily dispersed in the air. It is more likely that ragweed, which blooms at the same time as the more conspicuous goldenrod, is the culprit.

The thorns of brambles invading shrub plantings can provide painful surprises, and so can those of thistle and horsenettle. In lawns the prickly seedpods of burclover or sandbur act as sharp reminders that those weeds are present and should be eliminated. A burclover seedpod can even puncture a bicycle tire! Anyone who has ever brushed against the brittle tubular hairs of stinging nettles knows enough to stay clear of them next time—and to control them.

Although there are harmful substances in many plants, cultivated and uncultivated, truly poisonous plants are rare. Raw ripening groundcherry fruit, jimsonweed leaves and seeds, pokeweed roots, and the colorful berries of nightshades, like many wild mushrooms, are weeds that should certainly not be eaten. Instruct children not to eat anything that is not ordinarily served at the table. A poisonous plant's potential hazard depends on a combination of factors, including the strength of the toxin, its concentration within plant parts, the amount actually swallowed, and the degree of sensitivity of the person. Poisonous weeds that have been allowed to grow to maturity pose the most potential

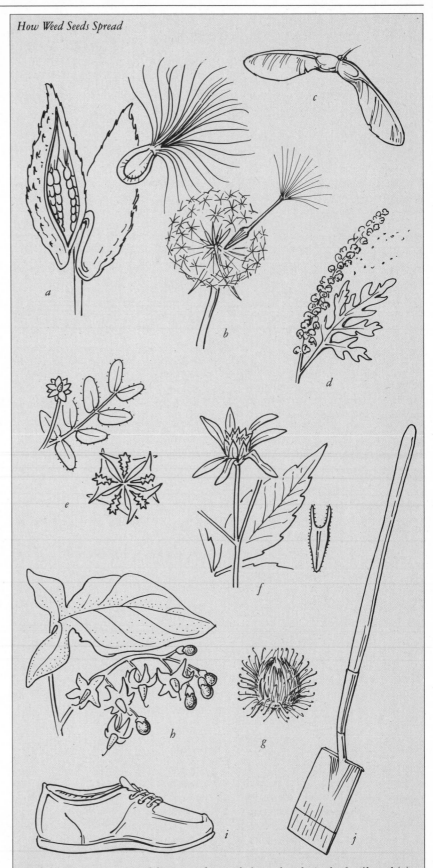

How Weed Seeds Spread

Weeds have ingenious ways of dispersing their seeds far and wide. Seeds of milkweed (a) and dandelion (b) float on wind currents with their silky hairs. Maple seeds (c) are sent spinning by their propellerlike wings. Ragweed seeds (d) scatter as they drop from shattered seedpods. Puncturevine (e), beggartick (f), and burdock (h) have barbs or spines that can attach to clothing, animal fur, or any other moving object and hitchhike for miles. Birds and other animals may eat tasty fruits, such as nightshade (g), spreading fruit seeds. People can spread weed seeds by moving soil about on a shoe (i) or a spade (j).

for such trouble making. Poisoning in the form of nausea or dizziness is more common than are more serious effects.

Weeds Look Untidy

Last but not least, weeds usually look bad. They're an affront to a gardener's pride because a weedy garden proclaims that it is a neglected garden. Weeds can mar the enjoyment of viewing a lawn and garden. Green garlic leaves poking up through brown dormant bermudagrass, bindweed garlanding rose bushes, thistles destroying the line of a low ground cover, crabgrass and nutsedge outgrowing the lawn, or dandelions gaily blooming amidst the turfgrass—all proclaim to neighbors and visitors that we haven't done what New Englanders call "our bounden duty."

WHY DO WEEDS SUCCEED?

Weeds are notorious plants that are able to survive, persist, and multiply even under adverse conditions. How do they do it? Amazingly versatile, their capacity to reproduce by many methods is a large part of the answer.

Weed Seeds

Consider their seeds, for instance. Most weeds can produce enormous amounts of seeds that are usually deposited on or in the soil. Some seeds remain on the surface; others are buried by earthworms and insects, washed beneath the surface, or turned under by a gardener hoeing the garden. Often the smaller and lighter the seed, the more is produced by a weed plant. By actual count single plants of common ragweed and Pennsylvania smartweed have been documented to produce over 3,000 seeds each. Pigweed is much worse, producing nearly 120,000 seeds per plant. This enormous seed-producing potential is surpassed by other weeds that fortunately are not encountered under home conditions.

In addition to their vast numbers, weed seeds generally have a high degree of viability. That is, most of them are capable of germinating when conditions are right—when moisture, light, and temperatures are favorable. Some seeds deteriorate but others stay alive a long, long time—for decades and perhaps a century or more, particularly if they are buried. In an experiment begun in 1879 in Michigan, bottles of buried seeds are dug up every 10 years and tested. Eighty years later curly dock, evening primrose,

and moth mullein were still able to germinate. Seeds of redroot pigweed, Virginia pepperweed, broadleaf plantain, and purslane remained alive for 40 years.

If you multiply the number of weed seeds that a mature weed might produce each year by the number of years the weed has been a problem and, assuming that most of those seeds have the ability to stay quietly in the soil until they can germinate, you begin to realize what a tremendous reservoir of weed seeds is in the soil. That's why you see so many new weeds when you cultivate or disturb the soil—you are bringing dormant seeds to the soil surface where they can readily germinate.

Sometimes people get discouraged about weediness, especially in lawns, and think they can correct the situation by digging up the lawn or garden and starting all over again—but it doesn't work that way. Disturbing the soil brings more weed seeds to the surface where they can germinate and continue the problem.

Invasion Tactics

Weeds have other tricks for reproducing and spreading. This is especially so with perennial weeds, the ones that keep on living year after year. Weeds like bermudagrass, ground ivy and white

clover spread and reproduce by stolons—creeping aboveground stems. Take a careful look and notice that besides forming mats, these stems root as they creep. The rooting is usually at a node, where leaves are attached and branches often form. Older parts of the weed may be eliminated, but if bits of rooted stem remain, they will continue to grow and increase the size of the patch.

This creeping can also go on underground by a type of stem called a rhizome. Canada thistle and quackgrass are major examples. Canada thistle has an interlaced system of rebranching vertical and horizontal rhizomes with buds that can produce shoots and roots within a couple of months after seedlings have germinated. This explains how a single thistle plant can quickly form a whole colony. Cultivating the site breaks up the rhizomes and stimulates the growth of many buds. It is hard to avoid cutting the rhizomes and every piece with a node that is left behind can start another new plant. Fortunately, Canada thistle seldom produces seeds because its flowers are imperfect and function either as male pollen-bearers or female seed-producers, not both. Colonies tend to be solely either male or female and so do not produce seeds.

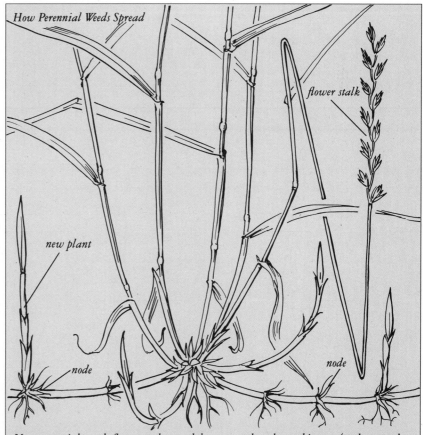

How Perennial Weeds Spread

flower stalk

new plant

node

node

Most perennial weeds flower and set seed, but many also rely on rhizomes (underground stems) to increase their numbers. Quackgrass is a good example. Although its rhizomes are shallow, they spread extensively and send up new plants from the nodes.

Quackgrass, on the other hand, spreads by both seeds and rhizomes. As with Canada thistle, a small piece of quackgrass rhizome with a node can start a new plant. You won't have to dig deeply to find out what quackgrass is doing underground because it is rather shallow-rooted. However, you may be amazed to see the extensive mat of branched chaffy-looking rhizomes it produces—tufts of fibrous roots are attached to each node and shoots emerge from many of these. An old-time farmer used to joke that he could shake a whole field by grasping and shaking the quackgrass in one corner.

The tips of quackgrass roots are nearly as hard as ivory, and they can penetrate tubers or other thickened stems encountered as they grow. More than one gardener has dug up potatoes that were pierced by quackgrass rhizomes so that they resembled big beads strung on a string.

Dandelions are by far the most common weed in American lawns. Many people find a good deal of satisfaction in removing the rosettes of leaves by cutting them out with a knife or other sharp instrument. This is only a temporary solution because the numerous, otherwise dormant buds on their taproots quickly surge into active growth. A dandelion's long taproot grips the soil and resists mighty efforts to dislodge it.

Gardeners experience a similar short-lived satisfaction in pulling up the shiny green tufts of nutsedge leaves that grow faster than the lawn grasses through which they emerge. The nutsedge tops come off easily enough but leave behind their assurance of a future in the form of little tubers or nutlets. Slender rhizomes radiate out from the basal mother bulb, and at varying distances from that base each one develops new bulbs at the tips. Bulbs form whether or not the initial clump of leaves is removed, increasing the stand of nutsedge.

Removing the main plant may stimulate the appearance of new tops and increase the weed problem. Pulling the leaves (and this is very easy to do) signals the nutlets to promptly sprout new leaves, and there are soon more nutsedge plants than before. If you are feeling particularly vindictive you can dig up a batch of the nutlets and roast and eat them, as they are quite tasty and are used as food in Africa, their original home. (Don't, of course, eat nutlets from a lawn that has recently been treated with a pesticide.)

Weeds As Pioneers

Some weeds survive by adapting to conditions under which little else can grow. It is difficult for most plants to grow in soil that has become compacted by constant foot traffic or other pressure or by being worked when it was too wet. This is especially true of clay soils, which have fine particles and little air space between them. Goosegrass and knotweed can tolerate such a condition and are often found growing along footpaths or on tennis courts and other sports fields where there is much trampling. These weeds also appear along driveways and in unpaved parking sites where little else survives.

Weeds often appear in other situations that limit the growth of most plants. Nutsedge tolerates poor drainage so well that it is often called watergrass. Moss is frequently found in damp, shady places, particularly if the soil is acid, and there are few soils so poor that ragweed can't grow in them. Even along gravelly roadsides and cindered railroads, which are constructed to discourage intrusive plants that could create a fire hazard or interfere with visibility, weeds survive.

WHERE DO WEEDS COME FROM?

It is important to realize that the presence of weeds is directly related to our own activities and that they appear when the native vegetation is disturbed. This is true of the areas cleared for homes and especially for those garden areas where we plant and nurture flowers, vegetables, fruits, and lawns. The balance of nature changes as factors in it change. However, without our interference native plants have settled down to fairly stable communities based on common environmental conditions such as temperature, rainfall and soil. Wild areas may be shaded forests, open fields, grassy prairies, or deserts. Wherever we disturb these communities and cultivate edible or ornamental plants, especially those not naturally adapted to the particular growing conditions, the aggressiveness and survival versatility of weeds become a problem.

Turning the soil brings dormant weed seeds to the surface where they can germinate. The first to appear are mostly annual weeds.

In disturbed soil a general sequence of weeds appears. The first year brings mostly annual grasses, such as crabgrass and foxtail, and some annual broadleaf weeds, such as ragweed, purslane, lambsquarters, smartweed, chickweed, and mustard. If the area is kept continuously cultivated, it will pretty much stay at this stage, although a few perennials such as bindweed, bermudagrass, nutsedge, or sorrel may creep in.

How do these weeds get there? Usually by unintentional means. Animal bedding and straw and especially hay used for cushioning cargo shipments are primary sources. Walk along a railroad or harbor dock, especially in unloading areas, and see how many familiar weeds are growing there. The seeds of whatever was growing with the straw or hay—ragweed, smartweed, mustard, or other weed—came right along, as did seeds of the hay crop itself.

Weeds, especially perennial ones but also seeds of annuals, can travel with live plants. Weeds often come along with plants bought in nursery containers, with divisions from a friend's garden, or from one part of the yard to another. Seeds can travel on muddy feet, animal fur, or clothing. Pieces of stem capable of forming roots often get caught on mowers, cultivators, or other implements and are spread that way. The same thing can happen with weed seeds, so be careful to keep your tools clean.

In the past weed seeds were commonly introduced as impurities with desired seeds but this happens far less often now. Inspections and statements of weed content on seed packages are required to prevent this very thing. Weed seeds are much more likely already to be in the soil from previous years; prodigious amounts of seeds lie dormant in most soils waiting to be brought near the soil surface where light, moisture, and temperature conditions are favorable for germination. This fact suggests that shallow cultivation is better than deep cultivation because it exhausts the supply of weed seeds near the surface and avoids bringing more seeds from deeper in the ground.

Wind spreads some weed seeds. Familiar gossamer parachutes carry dandelion seeds hither and yon. Other seeds are spread by water washing them from where they were originally dropped. They may travel down cracks in the soil or float with the current. A few plants have a fascinating mechanism for forcibly ejecting their seeds when they are ripe so that they land at some distance from their parent. Oxalis has the ability to shoot its seeds as far as 6 feet away.

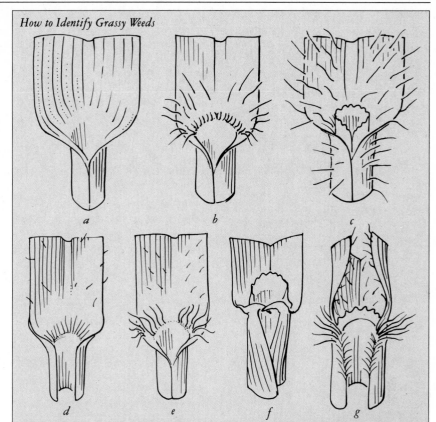

How to Identify Grassy Weeds

The collar of a grass leaf—where the leaf meets the stem—offers an excellent clue to identification. Some collars may be smooth, bristly, or hairy, and others may feature a dry papery bract. The most common grassy weeds are barnyardgrass (a), yellow foxtail (b), large crabgrass (c), fall panicum (d), bermudagrass (e), quackgrass (f), goosegrass (g).

Insects help disperse many seeds, often carrying them away for food. Birds spread them far and wide. Animals and people move seeds too, if the seeds get caught on fur or clothing. That's how sticktights got their common name. The burs of cocklebur are notorious for hitching a ride on any form of convenient transportation.

PLANT RELATIONSHIPS

As with garden plants weeds can be classified into groups and families according to their biological similarities. These similarities become important when controlling weeds and explain their different responses to various herbicide treatments. Scientists exploit these differences when developing control methods.

Weeds may either be grassy, belonging to the grass family, or broadleaf. Broadleaf weeds usually have broad flat leaves with veins forming a lacy network. Their internal structures, especially those for moving nutrients and water, are different from grasses.

The many grassy weeds can be difficult to tell apart. For positive identification flowers and seeds may be needed, but leaf characteristics can usually help gardeners distinguish the many common species. The handiest clues are in the small area, called the collar, where the flat leaf blade angles away from the stem. The collar often contains projections called ligules. Ligules may be delicate, smooth-edged membranes, or membranes with a jagged edge. They may consist of coarse or fine hairs, or be nonexistent. Hairs, or the lack of them, on the blade itself help with the identification too. (Some of the most common grassy weeds are compared in the illustration above.)

It often takes a very close look for a gardener to distinguish one grass from another, but knowing which is which can mean the difference between effective weed control and rampant weed growth.

It is especially important to know which group of plants a weed belongs to when choosing an appropriate herbicide. Herbicides alter the way plants grow, and grasses and broadleaf plants behave differently. These differences mean that herbicides are often selective. One group of plants may be sensitive to or respond to a compound that does not affect the other and vice versa. (A more detailed discussion of selectivity appears on pages 17 and 18.)

WEED LIFE CYCLES

Although plants have evolved into many different forms with diverse structures and ways of reproducing, most familiar garden plants and weeds reproduce by forming seeds. Some plants can also reproduce from pieces of root or stem.

Higher plants have one of three types of life cycles: annual, biennial, or perennial, although this can vary depending upon the climate. Annual bluegrass, for instance, in a cool moist climate often behaves as a perennial. In the South some weeds that are biennial elsewhere may mature faster and behave as winter annuals. Understanding a weed's life cycle helps a gardener learn how to control the weed.

Annuals

Within a single year, annual weeds germinate, flower, form seeds, and complete their lives. Most annuals do this between spring and fall. These are sometimes referred to as summer annuals. Pigweed, ragweed, and crabgrass are well-known annual weeds. Another group, referred to as winter annuals, prefers cool weather. These weeds germinate in the fall and continue growing until hot weather arrives the following spring, when they set seed and die. Henbit, common chickweed, cress, and annual bluegrass usually behave this way. Knowing how these annual weeds behave provides one more clue to controlling them—the earlier in their life cycle the better.

Preventing annual weeds from forming seeds is an important element in controlling them. Purslane, spurge, and galinsoga, for instance, are especially prolific because they flower and produce large amounts of seeds only a few weeks after they germinate. New seedlings sprout, flower, and set seed all season long; often a whole series of generations is growing side by side by summer's end.

Biennials

Although biennials are similar to annuals, they need two years to complete their lives. They spend the first year as a rosette of leaves close to the ground; the second year they send up a shoot that produces flowers and seeds. Bull thistle and wild carrot are common biennial weeds. It is easiest to interrupt the growth of such plants by eliminating the less conspicuous rosettes their first year. In warm climates some biennials may act as cool-season annuals.

Perennials

Either herbaceous or woody, perennials live for at least three years. Roots or bulbs of herbaceous perennials remain alive even though the tops may die to

Top left: If a perennial weed stores energy in its roots, it can grow back quickly if only the growth aboveground is removed. This curly dock has resprouted from a buried taproot.

Top middle: This curly dock plant has sprouted from a fragment of perennial taproot, which is still visible at the bottom of the root system.

Top right: A curly dock seedling grows slower than a root sprout, since it lacks root-stored food.

Bottom: A sea of yellow mustard flowers is striking, but it announces that this annual weed is about to release thousands of troublesome seeds.

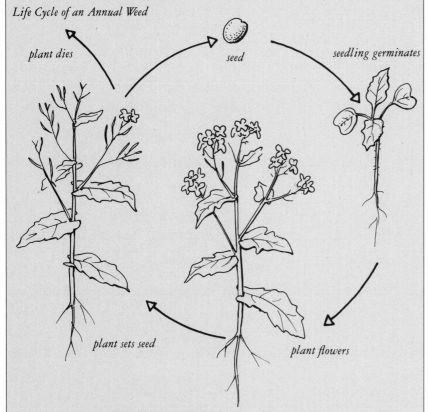

Life Cycle of an Annual Weed

plant dies

seed

seedling germinates

plant sets seed

plant flowers

An annual weed, such as the mustard illustrated here, completes its entire life cycle in a single growing season. Seeds are the only way an annual weed survives from one year to the next. Interrupt that cycle by preventing seed set and weed problems will diminish.

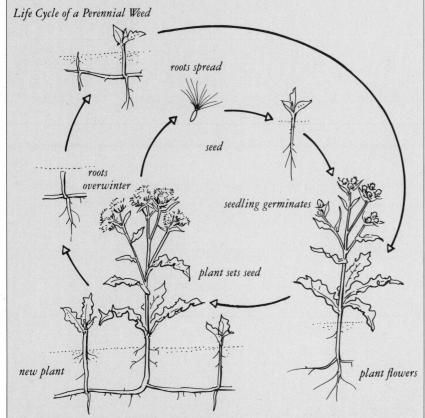

Life Cycle of a Perennial Weed

roots spread

seed

roots overwinter

seedling germinates

plant sets seed

new plant

plant flowers

A perennial weed, such as the Canada thistle illustrated here, lives from year to year. Its tops die down at the end of each growing season, but the roots overwinter and send up shoots the next year. Seeds can begin new plants but roots or spreading rhizomes, which can form new plants, increase the size of the weed colony. Effective control means interrupting flowering as well as killing the entire system of roots or rhizomes.

the ground in winter. After a dormant period new growth emerges from the roots. Woody perennials (shrubs, vines, and trees) develop woody tissue that persists year after year.

Perennial weeds often spread and form colonies by sending up new plants from rhizomes or stolons. They can calso increase by seed. Whether herbaceous or woody, perennials keep growing, but the time they flower and form seeds is restricted to one relatively short period each year.

Choosing Control Methods

When a perennial weed flowers and forms seeds, it draws on energy that comes largely from starches and sugars already stored in its roots. This gives you a tip about control. Application of herbicides or mechanical control techniques often work best on perennial weeds if used at the end of the growing season when the plant is storing food in the roots. At this time the sugary plant sap is moving downward into the roots and can carry the herbicide along with it. Herbicides are also effective during seasons when stored food is depleted.

Weeds that continue some growth over a long season—honeysuckle, for example—can often be controlled best when desirable plants are dormant. They can then be treated without harming the garden plants among which they are growing. This technique is described in the second chapter, Using Herbicides Safely and Effectively.

Annual weeds usually predominate in areas kept constantly cultivated. Perennial weed seedlings may soon follow annuals and dominate if allowed to. Take advantage of dormant periods to dig out the roots of perennial weeds if you haven't gotten them under control as they've initially appeared—by far the best time to do that. The rhizomes of quackgrass, for example, are vulnerable to cold and turning them up during the winter may eliminate the weed, especially if you remove sprouts that attempt regrowth in the spring.

Being vigilant and keeping annual or perennial weeds from becoming firmly established and sending out their roots or spreading their seeds can prevent them from ever becoming a major problem. It's the old story of an ounce of prevention being worth a pound of cure.

USING HERBICIDES SAFELY AND EFFECTIVELY

Wishing, no matter how fervently, for weeds to disappear from the garden won't do the trick. However, modern science has provided a kind of magic weeding wand in the form of chemicals called herbicides. These compounds kill plants. The most amazing of them can eliminate certain plants without harming others, an ability referred to as selectivity.

This chemical magic has become possible only within about the past 40 years as scientists learned more and more of the fine details of how plants grow and especially about the naturally occurring chemicals within them that direct their growth. Modern herbicides that resemble natural plant hormones can control weeds and save gardeners a great deal of time and wearying labor.

Used on lawns and in gardens, certain herbicides prevent the appearance of crabgrass. Other herbicides neatly eliminate lawn weeds already present without killing the desirable turfgrass. When applied properly some herbicides keep weeds from appearing among bedding plants or in freshly cultivated ground under shrubs. A careful check of product labels confirms that some herbicides can be used to control weeds growing in established beds of ornamental plants and even in vegetable gardens. However, using herbicides among established ornamentals and vegetables is tricky because gardens usually have a diverse selection of plants with great differences in the ways they respond.

Weed killer in a ready-to-use applicator allows cleanup of weed problems with a minimum of fuss. This nonselective herbicide will kill grassy or broadleaf weeds in the cracks of a walkway.

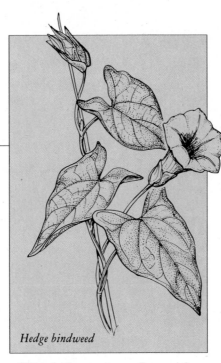

Hedge bindweed

With lawn and garden weed killers, controlling weeds can be easy, efficient, and effective. This chapter explains the different ways herbicides work and tells you which herbicides to use and how to apply them correctly.

Eliminating brush and undesirable woody plants with herbicides is more efficient and can be safer than any other control method. For example, hand-pulling poison ivy or poison oak gives many people a serious rash and most likely leaves viable roots behind; spraying these weeds with an herbicide can eliminate the problem without your ever touching the plant. Tree seedlings that sprout in beds of shrubs or ground covers can be eliminated without harming the desirable plants by using the right herbicide the right way. It is easy to prevent unsightly weeds from growing between the bricks or stones of a patio, in gravelled driveways or paths, under fences, in tennis courts, or other places where you don't want anything growing. Again, it is simply a matter of choosing the appropriate herbicide and using it as the label directs.

READ THE LABEL

To use herbicides safely and effectively, the first basic principle is to *read the label*, reading it carefully and reading it more than once. Read the label before buying the herbicide, read it before mixing the product, and check directions before applying it. Afterward read it again before storing any that is left, and finally before disposing of the empty container or any leftover product. Be sure you understand the nature of the herbicide you are going to use, and any precautions that should be taken.

Every pesticide label must be approved and registered by the Environmental Protection Agency (EPA) before the product may be sold. Each label carries the statement, "It is a violation of Federal law to use the product in a manner inconsistent with its labeling." This is a protection and a warning against trying to second-guess the manufacturer.

The product label is the basic source of detailed information about an herbicide. Read the entire label very carefully even though the print may be fine and some of the terms unfamiliar. The label directions will tell you how to use the product so that it performs as the manufacturer intended. A great deal of research went into determining the information on the label, so read it and follow the directions exactly. The EPA requires some of the label statements for your safety.

Active Ingredients

When choosing an herbicide, the first thing to look for on the label after the trade name of the product is the brief description of what it does—what kinds of weeds you can expect it to control in which garden areas. Next look to see what active ingredients it contains. Active ingredients are the part of a product that do the weed killing. These ingredients are always listed on the front of the label and include the chemical name (the long scientific name) of the active ingredient or ingredients and usually the shorter official common name. The percentage of active and inert ingredients is also listed.

Either name, chemical or common, will help you relate the product to your state's recommendations. The cooperative extension service in each county publishes recommendations for the use of herbicides and other pesticides based on state laws and conditions. Fliers or pamphlets are available at no charge or for a small fee; unbiased advice based on local research and experience is also available. Recommendations are usually given in terms of chemical compounds, rather than commercial product trade names.

Directions for Use

Use an herbicide only in the garden areas and on the crops or plants listed on the label. It might call for using the product on lawns, around ornamentals, in a vegetable garden, or in nonfood-crop areas. The label also includes a listing of weeds the product will control.

The rest of the label has additional directions for safe and effective use, such as avoiding unfavorable weather conditions or very sensitive plants. It provides the proper dilution or rate of application for the area to be treated. The best time for treatment and directions for repeat applications are also given.

Read the label so you will know what to expect from the product and how and where to use it. The place for experimentation is in the laboratory, not in the backyard. Follow the label directions to avoid harming your valuable plants.

Safety Instructions

Every chemical, even household cleansers and detergents, have some degree of potential hazard to people. The front panel of the herbicide label carries a signal word in large letters to let you know what that product's potential hazard is. These signal words are *caution,* which means the product is slightly toxic; *warning,* which means it is moderately toxic; and *danger,* which means it is highly toxic and extra care should be taken when using it. *Danger—poison* with skull and crossbones appears on labels of products that can cause human or animal death if ingested or inhaled; use of these pesticides is restricted to licensed professional applicators only. Such products are no longer available to home gardeners. Sometimes the herbicide's concentration in the product helps determine which signal word appears on the label. For instance, a ready-to-use product might be labeled *caution* while a concentrated version of the same product that requires dilution might state *warning.*

Labels carry precautionary statements to ensure that they are used safely. These include mention of any potential health hazard, such as avoiding contact that might cause eye irritation; environmental hazard, such as toxicity to fish; ways to avoid contact with nontarget plants; and what to do in case of accident. Directions for storing or disposing of unused product also appear on the label. There is always a reminder on the front to keep containers out of the reach of children.

HERBICIDES WORK IN DIFFERENT WAYS

Modern herbicides vary in their chemical characteristics and thus in the way plants respond to them. Many are selective, meaning they affect certain plants but leave others unharmed. Some herbicides are nonselective and can injure or kill nearly any weed or garden plant to which they are applied.

Both selective and nonselective herbicides work in one of two ways—by killing the tissue they contact or by being absorbed and moving throughout the plant. Contact herbicides rapidly kill the plant tissues they touch but do not move further into the plant. Methanearsonates, used for controlling crabgrass in lawns,

Study the label of any herbicide before buying the product and again before using it. Follow the directions exactly. This sample label shows how typical information is arranged under several headings to help locate the details needed.

PRECAUTIONARY STATEMENTS
HAZARDS TO HUMANS AND DOMESTIC ANIMALS
CAUTION _____

ENVIRONMENTAL HAZARDS _____

PHYSICAL OR CHEMICAL HAZARDS _____

READ ENTIRE LABEL. USE STRICTLY IN ACCORDANCE WITH LABEL PRECAUTIONS AND DIRECTIONS. _____

CONTROLS THE FOLLOWING WEEDS _____

HOW TO USE _____

WHERE TO USE _____

WHEN TO APPLY _____

NOTE _____

STORAGE AND DISPOSAL _____

STORAGE _____

— PRODUCT —

— CONTAINER —

NOTICE _____

Chevron Chemical Co.
Ortho Consumer products Division

E.P.A. Reg No. ___

0283417301

C

Chevron

ORTHO

WEED KILLER

READY TO USE - NO MIXING

CONTROLS _____

ACTIVE INGREDIENTS _____

INERT INGREDIENTS _____

Keep Out of Reach of Children
CAUTION
See back panel for additional precautionary statements
Net Contents 8 Fl. oz.

are selective contact herbicides; when used according to label directions they do not kill the turfgrass, but only the treated crabgrass foliage. Although the crabgrass roots are not killed, the crabgrass eventually dies because the tops are burnt back and the weed cannot resprout. Systemic herbicides translocate or move throughout a plant, their toxic effects often appearing at a distance from where they were absorbed. For instance 2,4-D is a well-known selective systemic herbicide; applied to a lawn it kills dandelions, roots and all, without harming the turf.

Glyphosate is a nonselective systemic herbicide; applied to foliage it slowly kills almost any plant. Paraquat is a nonselective contact herbicide used by licensed professional applicators to kill any plant to which it is applied.

Most herbicides, whether selective or nonselective, are postemergent herbicides; they control weeds when applied to foliage—which, of course, appears after the weeds emerge from the soil. Some herbicides work best when applied to the soil, where they interfere with seed germination or seedling growth. This type of treatment is termed preemergent. A selective preemergent, such as DCPA (Dacthal®), can be applied to a lawn to prevent crabgrass from germinating in spring. A nonselective preemergent, such as prometon, kills all vegetation and keeps on preventing it for up to a year.

Contact Herbicides

Contact herbicides appear to burn foliage on treated plants but the effect is limited to the tissue actually touched by the spray. Since contact herbicides do not move from one plant part to another, it's important to cover the entire weed with the spray. Otherwise, untreated sections continue to grow, just as if you had merely broken off part of the plant.

A contact herbicide only temporarily controls perennial weeds; although it kills the top, the weed usually resprouts from its uninjured roots. A contact herbicide usually completely kills annual weeds because annuals don't have the regenerative capability of perennials.

Systemic Herbicides

Plant growth regulators—systemic herbicides—act to disrupt normal plant growth processes. When absorbed by roots, foliage, or bark, they move throughout the plant and produce their effect elsewhere. Some affect a plant's

enzymes, others increase respiration and carbohydrate use. The result is evident in swollen stems, twisted and deformed leaves, and eventually a dead plant. Others inhibit cell division, disrupt membranes, or interfere with root growth.

It may take a week or even a month for the growth-damaging effects to become apparent. If the application is too light, a repeat application may further upset a plant system that is already out of whack and produce the desired kill. However, an overdose of systemic herbicide may kill surface cells too quickly and prevent further movement of the weed killer into the plant, preventing it from doing its job. With these herbicides the old adage "if a little is good, then

Top: Lawn or weeds growing under a young tree seriously slow its growth. Here an herbicide was used to clear a circle, which can later be covered with mulch. Bottom: Weeds treated with hormone-type herbicides exhibit epinasty—elongation and twisting of stems and leaves. This dandelion was treated with 2,4-D several days before the photograph was taken.

more is better" is not true. An application rate different from that intended can produce a different effect.

HERBICIDE SELECTIVITY

Although salt, ashes, and oils have been used for centuries to control weeds, until the 1940s attempts to kill weeds chemically were nonselective and not very satisfactory. Common table salt, by absorbing moisture from soil and plant tissues, kills weeds but also most other nearby plants. It leaves asparagus and onions unscathed, however, when applied to the soil at a rate of 20 tons per acre. To control roadside weeds with oil, 100 to 300 gallons must be applied to every acre. Chemicals such as copper salts, iron sulfate, and sodium arsenite were once used to kill certain broadleaf weeds without killing cereal crops. The best compounds were too bulky, corrosive, or dangerous to handle.

The revolution in weed science began with the study of plant growth hormones during the 1930s. Scientists discovered

Selective herbicides control either broadleaf or grassy plants without damaging plants of the opposite type. Here grassy weeds are killed without harm to nearby rose bushes.

that just a few ounces of the hormone 2,4-D applied per acre controlled broadleaf weeds in lawns and pastures and left the grasses unscathed. 2,4-D was the first truly selective herbicide—and it was readily and economically applied.

All plants contain various growth-regulating chemicals or hormones. Once researchers discovered the chemical makeup of many of these compounds, they were able to create synthetic compounds that produced similar effects. Such compounds act as plant growth regulators and make effective herbicides. Manufacturing these compounds in a laboratory is far more economical than extracting the natural compounds.

The well-known 2,4-D, the similar MCPP (mecoprop), and 2,4-DP (dichlorprop) and the closely related triclopyr are selective herbicides that act as plant growth regulators. When treated, stems of sensitive plants become twisted and swollen, foliage grows into malformed fingerlike leaves with veins closer together than usual, and extra secondary roots often sprout from the stem. Plants that are not sensitive to the hormone show no growth effects.

The characteristics of each modern herbicide have been studied under laboratory and field conditions by researchers who observe which plants respond to the treatment and which do not. The researchers determine the proper rate of application and when it should be applied. Product labels list plants controlled by the herbicide and tell which garden situations are appropriate for its use. Read the label and follow the directions when choosing an appropriate herbicide to use in each type of situation.

What Determines Selectivity?

Herbicides work in many ways—ways as complex and varied as the many life processes of the plants they control. Several major factors help determine selectivity. One of the most conspicuous is whether the plant to be treated is a monocot, meaning a member of the grass family, or a dicot, meaning a broadleaf plant (see page 11).

Several herbicides control most plants in one of these groups but not in the other. The ability of 2,4-D and MCPP to kill dandelions and other broadleaf weeds in a lawn without killing the grass is a good example of this kind of selectivity. The actual species of grass being treated can also make a difference. For instance, St. Augustine grass and bentgrass tend to be more sensitive to 2,4-D than bluegrass and most other turfgrasses; the sensitive grasses tolerate treatment only with a low concentration of the herbicide. Although most broadleaf plants are affected by 2,4-D, a few lawn weeds including violets and perennial speedwells (veronicas) do not respond to most lawn herbicides and are thus resistant.

Whether or not a plant is woody may influence selectivity. Also, waxy or hairy leaf surfaces can make it difficult for the herbicide to enter the foliage. Properly formulated products usually compensate for these potential problems.

The concentration, type of formulation, and amount of product applied can influence selectivity by producing a greater or lesser effect on the treated plants (see page 17).

Environmental Factors and Selectivity

The stage and rate of growth of weeds and garden plants also can influence the effectiveness of an herbicide's selectivity. Growing weeds, whose cells are dividing rapidly, usually are more readily affected than mature weeds, whose tissues have hardened and whose cells are no longer dividing. It helps to be aware of this when treating crabgrass, for example, and most other annual weed species.

Not all weeds are most sensitive when they are just beginning active growth—perennials, for example, are not most sensitive at this time. This may be because a systemic herbicide moves through a plant along with the sugars it uses for food. During the weed's initial growth in spring, food reserves are moving primarily upward from the roots. The herbicide may kill some of the top growth, but because it doesn't move easily downward into the plant, regrowth from roots and stems may occur.

Late in the growing season, food moves downward to replace those reserves; at this time an herbicide is readily carried throughout the plant and is most effective. Many woody plants respond better to glyphosate or triclopyr as the season advances. Poison ivy and Japanese honeysuckle do not respond well until they have used up enough stored food to have developed their first mature leaves.

Because herbicides affect a plant's growth mechanisms, it follows that the rate at which the plant is growing is another factor influencing selectivity. If growing conditions are good and plants (whether desirable plants or weeds) are actively growing, the degree of selectivity will be greater.

Weeds in a lawn stressed by lack of water during a drought won't respond as well to herbicide treatment because they aren't growing actively enough. The grass, which is also growing slowly, will be more sensitive to the treatment and may be injured. This means that selectivity is reduced, weed control is poor, and the lawn itself may be hurt. The same thing may happen where soil fertility is too low to support good plant growth. When growing conditions are good, weed control and turf safety are both improved.

PREEMERGENT CONTROL

The familiar adage "an ounce of prevention is worth a pound of cure" was never truer than in controlling weeds. Preemergent herbicides applied to the soil before weed seeds germinate prevent messy, competitive weeds from ever appearing aboveground. Use of these herbicides can prevent hours of hand-pulling, hoeing, spraying, and perhaps reseeding later in the growing season. Benefin, bensulide, trifluralin, dichlobenil, and DCPA (Dacthal®) are all reliable and readily available preemergents for homeowner use.

Preemergent herbicides are most commonly applied to lawns to keep crabgrass and other weedy grasses from appearing. However, some chemicals, especially DCPA (Dacthal®) and trifluralin, can be used on clean-cultivated soil before or immediately after planting ornamentals or vegetables. These chemicals are especially useful around newly planted shrubbery and ground covers that will need time to fill in and effectively shade out any weeds.

It is also possible to make a preemergent application to certain established plants. DCPA, dichlobenil, and trifluralin can be used this way around certain ornamental and vegetable plants. Check the label carefully to see which plants are listed.

Proper timing is crucial to the initial effectiveness of preemergent herbicides—they can't control weeds that have already germinated, although they will prevent further germination for 60 to 90 days after treatment. In a garden it is necessary to free the surface of weeds by clean cultivating just before applying the herbicide. (Clean cultivation means to cultivate soil and remove all weeds and weed seedlings so only desirable plants are left. The preemergent won't control already growing weeds.) Then don't cultivate again until the herbicide loses its effectiveness and weeds begin to appear. (Trifluralin must be initially worked into the soil by cultivation or watering.) By leaving the herbicide in place, a barrier of herbicide remains to be absorbed by germinating seedlings, killing them well before they become established or even before they can emerge. If the barrier is broken by cultivation, the effectiveness is lost, although inserting small transplants isn't a problem as long as the rest of the treated soil isn't disturbed. A few weeds may escape; if so pull them out by hand.

Fumigants

Fumigants are temporary soil sterilants useful for killing practically all weed roots, rhizomes, and seeds, as well as nematodes, harmful insects, and disease organisms in the soil. Used before planting they act like super preemergent herbicides. Their use has very serious drawbacks, the primary one being that they are highly toxic.

Fumigants are not selective—they destroy beneficial insects and fungi, as well as roots of trees or other plants growing in the treated area. Fumigants are quite difficult for even professionals to apply properly and safely, and they are expensive.

Metham (Vapam®) is the only soil fumigant home gardeners may buy. The only really justifiable reason for using it is to control heavy infestations of such difficult-to-control weeds as nutsedge or bermudagrass before establishing a new lawn or vegetable garden. Since vegetables have different tolerances, using herbicides in a vegetable bed is often impractical.

Metham (Vapam®) must be watered or mixed into warm soil (minimum soil temperature 60° F), and then sealed in by heavy watering or with a plastic covering. The soil must be prepared carefully ahead of time and planting can't safely begin for two to four weeks after treatment.

Preemergent herbicides prevent weed seeds from germinating or kill very young weed seedlings, but they don't harm the desirable plants that are already growing in the garden.

POSTEMERGENT CONTROL

When annual or perennial weeds are already up and growing, the way to control them chemically is with a postemergent herbicide. Depending upon the site and the weed problem, either a selective or nonselective herbicide may be appropriate. Most selective herbicides used for postemergent application to foliage have a little preemergent activity in the soil surface. For instance, when controlling broadleaf weeds in a lawn with a systemic herbicide such as 2,4-D, the lawn should not be reseeded for two to four weeks because the herbicide can kill the grass seedlings.

Herbicides can be applied in one of two ways: broadcast or spot treatment. A broadcast treatment is made over a large area that often contains both weeds and desirable plants. In spot application only the weed is treated and desirable plants located near the weed must be shielded from the herbicide (see page 25).

Broadcast Treatment

A postemergent broadcast treatment works beautifully where weeds that are sensitive to a selective herbicide are growing in a stand of resistant plants—for example, dandelions and plantains growing in a lawn can be killed without harming the grass. Because the herbicide doesn't affect grasses an entire weed-infested lawn can be treated, a quicker process than treating weeds individually. As weed growth slowly responds to the herbicide's interference and disruption of its metabolism, you have the satisfaction of watching weeds deteriorate and finally disappear. In a few days herbicide symptoms are usually noticeable as yellowing or twisted leaves, although complete weed death takes longer, sometimes as long as two to three weeks.

When treating weeds with a systemic herbicide, be patient. Even if particularly resistant weeds do not seem to respond to the initial treatment, wait at least two weeks or the length of time directed on the label before treating again. Reapplying a selective herbicide to a lawn too soon may injure the turfgrass.

Any of the application equipment described beginning on the next page is suitable for broadcast treatment. Just be sure to apply the herbicide uniformly and at the rate directed on the label.

Spot Treatment

If a weed is well separated from other plants, you can direct a pinpoint spray right to the weed without letting any herbicide particles fall on desirable plants. Ready-to-use products work well this way.

When making directed spot treatments, your natural inclination will be to make sure that enough material gets on the unwanted foliage, but resist that impulse. An overdose can defeat your purpose by burning leaf tissue before enough active ingredient can enter the weed to control it. Some gardeners work out a technique for wiping an herbicide over the weed or dipping it into a solution, but these are not recommended unless registered by manufacturers and described on the label.

HERBICIDE FORMULATIONS

Herbicide products are usually processed into a form that is easy and effective to use. Active ingredients may be prepared in a dry granular formulation or as a liquid that is either concentrated or diluted to application strength. Certain active ingredients are formulated in different

Top: A lightweight plastic backpack sprayer works well broadcasting a liquid herbicide on a lawn. The spray pressure is maintained in this one by pumping a handle.
Bottom: Use a spot weeder on scattered weeds growing through gravel, pavement, or mulch. A foam marker indicates which weeds have been treated.

ways and are available in different concentrations, including ready-to-use products that need no further dilution.

The pure (technical grade) form of an herbicidal active ingredient is seldom suitable for direct application. For practical purposes it must be combined with other appropriate materials so that the ingredient itself can be diluted with water to the very low concentration needed for effective control and uniform distribution. Sometimes the active ingredient is impregnated on granules of an inert carrier or fertilizer for dry application.

A good formulation helps the herbicide kill weeds and stabilizes the chemicals so they reach the customer in the same condition they left the manufacturer. They should remain in that condition in storage and perform properly when applied.

An active ingredient is usually processed into a more easily used or effective form, making it easier to dilute and apply evenly. The type of formulation—

often indicated on the label as an ester, an amine, or another salt—can make a difference in your choice (see page 24).

Granular Herbicides

Many people like to use granular materials because they're easier to measure, they don't require any further mixing, and they are easy to spread uniformly since the granules are visible when applied. In general granular herbicides may be somewhat easier to apply than liquids and safer near sensitive ornamentals, but they work more slowly because the active ingredient must be dissolved to be absorbed by the weed.

With a preemergent, if rain isn't expected soon, it helps to irrigate the treated area after application. This dissolves the herbicide and gets it to the root zone, where it will have its effect. However, with a postemergent product, withhold watering for a day or two so the target weeds can absorb the weed killer before it is washed from the foliage.

Liquid Herbicides

There is a wider range of liquid formulation possibilities. The simplest to use are those completely soluble in water, such as glyphosate and salts of MCPP, dicamba, and 2,4-D. Such formulations have no significant volatility, which makes them safest to use (see page 25), although it is hard for them to penetrate waxy coverings on leaves. Rain within 12 hours of application may dilute them further or wash them off entirely.

Because of the chemical nature of some active ingredients, certain herbicides must be dissolved in oil to formulate them. When they are, an emulsifier is also added so the concentrate can be diluted with water. This is much like using soap to emulsify any oils when washing your hands. Such products are called emulsifiable concentrates (usually ester formulations) and are commonly used for increasing weed penetration or to formulate products that are not soluble in water. Their oily nature helps them penetrate leaf surfaces more quickly, so they remain effective even if it rains an hour or two after application.

To assure maximum weed-killing effectiveness, formulations may also include one or more wetting agents (surfactants). These help the product stick to and spread out on the plant surface rather than roll off or get caught by tiny leaf hairs. When expertly chosen by the formulator, these materials also help the herbicide penetrate leaf surfaces so it can get to work inside the plant.

Because good products contain appropriate additives in the proper balance, it is neither necessary nor advisable to add anything not directed on the label.

APPLICATION EQUIPMENT

No matter what kind of job you are doing, good tools can make a difference—controlling weeds is no exception. In fact, high-quality equipment is essential for applying the tiny amounts of active ingredients in an herbicide product accurately, uniformly, and at the required rate. Choose application equipment as carefully as you do the herbicide.

Spreaders

Granular materials of any kind, including herbicides, are usually applied with some kind of spreader. The simplest is the ready-to-use shaker canister. Simply shake the material out onto the ground at the rate recommended on the label. (Labels show a picture of particles on the soil to help you gauge the application rate.)

For covering large areas such as lawns, the most common spreader is the wheeled drop spreader. It has a hopper that holds the product, which falls through holes along the bottom. A trigger mounted on the handle controls the release of the herbicide as you walk at a steady pace.

Another type of lawn spreader is the rotary cyclone type, which shoots the granules out sideways from a spinning discharge plate. There are several variations. Mounted ones have a rotating disk propelled by a drive wheel that moves as you push the spreader forward. Another type can be slung over a shoulder and material is released by turning a handle. Lightweight handheld versions are handy for treating small areas and are easy to store. The pistol grip and trigger are operated with the one hand and the crank for the broadcast wheel with the other.

Application isn't quite as accurate with broadcast spreaders as with drop types but because they throw the material in a wide arc, they require fewer steps. Compensate for the fact that they apply somewhat more material in the center of the arc than on the edges by overlapping swaths just a little bit.

Top: The Whirlybird® *spreader is handy for small areas. Bottom: Drop lawn spreaders let you control the output of granular herbicides by adjusting the spreader's output and walking at a steady pace.*

To become familiar with a spreader's output, try a small amount first over a small area, walking at an easy steady pace. The label of a granular herbicide usually includes recommended settings for the more commonly available spreaders. These calculate how much material the spreader will apply to a given area, assuring that the right amount of material

Hose-end sprayers turn a garden hose into an herbicide applicator. Just add the right amount of herbicide and water to the plastic jar—water from the hose will further dilute it.

gets applied in the right spacing. Simply adjust the spreader to the proper setting and walk at a steady pace as the granules fall through. Be sure to shut the valve while turning around or stopping.

Always try to run out all the material in the hopper. Rinsing out and drying the spreader before it is put away helps prevent corrosion.

Sprayers

Gardeners have a wide choice of sprayers for applying liquid herbicides. The simplest is the pressurized aerosol can that is its own applicator. Just point and press the button to release prediluted herbicide exactly where you want it. The next step up is a ready-to-use prediluted liquid formulation in a container with a trigger sprayer. Its only drawback is that your hand may get tired pumping the trigger. You pay something for the convenience of these ready-to-use products, but you avoid the nuisance of diluting and mixing a concentrate. Ready-to-use products are handy for keeping all season to use whenever you want to spot-treat just a few weeds.

For liquid broadcast treatment of larger areas, a hose-end sprayer is inexpensive and convenient. The concentrated or slightly diluted herbicide goes into a plastic jar with a spray nozzle that screws onto the end of a garden hose. The herbicide is discharged through a nozzle on the jar as pressure in the hose adds water and further dilutes the product. When using a hose-end sprayer, it is important to move steadily and spray evenly so the application is as uniform as possible. If the water pressure is too high, turn down the volume at the faucet before applying the weed killer.

It helps to run a preliminary trial with just water to get a feel for how fast or slow to spray to get proper coverage. Most of the droplets from a hose-end sprayer are relatively large, but be careful to keep the nozzle pointed downward so any spray doesn't drift or hit nearby shrubbery or garden plants (see page 24).

Liquid herbicide concentrates can also be applied with several kinds of pressurized tank sprayers. The simplest is a small tank sprayer that is pumped much like a bicycle pump to create pressure. The 2- and 3-gallon sizes are easy to carry and

Calibrating a Sprayer

10 ft

10 ft

Before applying a liquid herbicide to a lawn or other large area, calculate the rate of application with plain water. Choose a 10- by 10-foot (100 sq ft) section of the driveway or other test area. Spray to evenly cover the area, then check to see how much water was applied. When diluting the herbicide, mix the amount of chemical needed to cover 100 square feet into the amount of water used on the test area. Then spray in the same manner as on the test area to get a correct application rate.

Always label equipment used for mixing and applying herbicides and don't use it for any other purpose. Accidental damage to desirable plants can occur from herbicide-contaminated equipment.

you soon learn how often to stop and pump to keep the pressure uniform. Somewhat more expensive but easier to use, especially if covering a large area, is the backpack tank sprayer that is worn like a knapsack. Ensure even pressure by steadily pumping a handle as you walk. With either of these the best choice of nozzle is one that produces a flat fan pattern of spray particles.

Empty the sprayer before putting it away; try to calculate ahead of time the amount of spray needed so none is left. If you have mixed too much, do not pour it down the drain or sewer. Spray out the remaining herbicide on weeds in unplanted areas. Then rinse the sprayer in three changes of fresh water, being sure that the wash water is emptied where it cannot harm valuable plants.

Most herbicide labels recommend that you keep a separate sprayer just for herbicides, not using it to apply fungicides or insecticides. This is because traces of herbicides left in the sprayer, even after rinsing several times in fresh water, could harm desirable plants. Sprayers can be cleaned by washing all parts thoroughly with trisodium phosphate, bleach, household ammonia, or activated charcoal, but this is usually not worth the trouble. It's easier to use separate sprayers. Be careful to mark the herbicide sprayer in a way that won't wear off.

GETTING THE MOST FROM AN HERBICIDE

Magic though they may seem, herbicides aren't total miracle workers. Desirable plants and weeds must be growing well for postemergent herbicides to be their most effective. Weather can influence herbicide activity in several ways. Poor growing conditions slow plant growth, making weeds harder to control and desirable plants more susceptible to injury. Rain can wash sprays off before they have a chance to work.

Effects of Weather

If rain or irrigation has been adequate and temperatures are fairly moderate, weeds and desirable plants (especially turfgrasses) will be growing well. The herbicide treatment can then most effectively disrupt weed growth and desirable resistant plants can most effectively tolerate the herbicide. When soil moisture is inadequate or temperatures excessively high or low, growth rates decrease—weeds become less responsive and desirable plants more vulnerable. There may be little or no weed control, or the response may be delayed until active growth resumes under more favorable conditions.

Applying postemergent herbicides in late summer or early fall—Labor Day or fairly soon afterward in most regions—has several advantages. Hard-to-kill perennial weeds often respond better then; apparently herbicides move into roots along with the food being stored. At that time of year, seedling weeds that have germinated throughout the summer will also be eliminated. Be sure, however, that the weather is warm enough when you apply the herbicide so that weeds are actively growing. This applies to spring applications too.

Postemergent herbicides have to be absorbed by plant tissue to be effective. The time required varies with the type of herbicide and also with the nature of the plant. If the herbicide is washed off the plant's foliage before it is fully absorbed or if it is leached below the soil level where it is needed, its effectiveness will be reduced or even lost. Before applying an herbicide, check the weather forecast and read the product label to see if the weather and herbicide are compatible.

Application Rates

Most herbicides are active in very small amounts and must be applied accurately if they're to work as they are intended. Dilute and apply the herbicide exactly as directed on the label. If too little is applied, the product won't control the weeds. Likewise if too much is applied, the herbicide may burn the foliage before enough of the chemical can be adequately absorbed—and again the weeds won't be controlled.

With herbicides it is essential to apply a given amount of chemical to a specified area. The amount of water used for diluting a preemergent herbicide can be varied considerably, but do not vary the recommended amount of chemical to apply to a given area. Changing the proportion could even produce a different plant response, so be careful. Estimate as accurately as you can the size of the area to be treated so you know how much ground you are going to cover with how much herbicide. It may be helpful to treat a small section at a time.

To become familiar with a sprayer's output, it is a good idea to calibrate it by testing with a premeasured amount of plain water on a 100-square-foot area (see opposite page). Walk at a comfortable speed and spray by crisscrossing, first from end to end and then from side to side. This helps avoid a miss or an overdose. After spraying the area, measure how much water is left. Determine the amount of water used by subtracting the amount that is left from the amount you started with. This tells you how much water to actually mix with the herbicide for every 100 square feet treated. (The label tells you how much concentrated herbicide to apply for a given area, such as 100 square feet.)

When applying dry herbicides check the spreader's output by treating a measured area from end to end and then from side to side (or measure according to label instructions) to make sure you distribute the proper amount of material evenly. If the spreader isn't calibrated properly, adjust the setting. With a drop spreader, overlap the wheel tracks to avoid missed or overdosed strips; with a cyclone spreader overlap the edge of the arcs to ensure even distribution.

AVOIDING OFF-TARGET ACCIDENTS

Careless use of herbicides can harm or even kill desirable plants. The key to using herbicides without damaging desirable plants is controlling where the herbicide is spread or sprayed. Be sure to apply it where you want it to go and only there. If you accidentally spray a desirable plant, rinse off the plant with water immediately.

Broadcast Application

Controlling where a broadcast spray lands and assuring spray uniformity is easiest with a nozzle that produces a flat fan-shaped pattern, rather than a solid or hollow cone-shaped one. When broadcasting a dry product, application is more uniform and more controlled with a properly calibrated drop spreader than with a cyclone spreader.

A few herbicides, especially long-lasting ones such as dicamba and prometon, can harm the roots of trees and shrubs. Do not apply these kinds of herbicides on slopes where runoff would occur, or to soil where roots might grow. It is best to assume that tree and shrub roots extend twice the height of the plant rather than to the edge of the drip line.

Spot Treatment

When weeds grow so close to desirable plants that even a neatly directed target spray might splash the foliage, extra precautions must be taken. Shield nearby sensitive plants with cardboard or similar material while spraying. This is sometimes easier if one person holds the shield while another sprays.

Controlling Drift

Next to careless application of herbicides to garden plants, the major culprit in herbicide accidents is drift—physical drift of tiny herbicide particles onto unintended plants or soil.

Protecting Desirable Plants

When spot-treating a weed growing close to a desirable plant, protect the plant from injury by shielding it from spray particles with a large piece of cardboard.

A good granular formulation won't have dust particles to drift, but watch the deposit pattern to be sure the granules aren't being flung or aren't bouncing or rolling farther than intended.

There is greater potential for drift with liquid materials. With their small particles sprays are readily blown off-target by even a light breeze. Spray drift can be controlled easily by keeping in mind a few commonsense precautions. Plan to spray when there is little or no air movement. Often the best time to spray is early in the morning or late in the afternoon when the air is relatively still.

Keep the spray nozzle fairly close to the ground, always pointing down and never waving the sprayer in the air. Check the nozzle opening occasionally to be sure it isn't clogged or hasn't become corroded. A damaged nozzle can change the spray rate and pattern, and it may produce some almost-invisible particles that could easily drift. Using too high a pressure does the same thing; turn down the volume at the faucet when using a hose-end sprayer.

Volatility

Under certain conditions, particularly extreme heat, certain liquid herbicides can evaporate and turn into vapor that drifts and injures desirable plants. Volatility, as this phenomenon is called, can cause trouble but is often blamed for injury that really results from careless application or spray drift.

Most substances are volatile under certain conditions; heat makes molecules move faster and turns solids into liquids and liquids into gases. Boiling water turns into steam and burning wood turns into smoke. With herbicides volatility is seldom significant except when a compound is formulated as an ester. Ester compounds work especially well on hard-to-kill weeds. The ingredient statement tells which type of formulation you are buying. Ester will be clearly indicated on the label, usually with the added fact that it is the low-volatile type now sold for home use.

Cool weather, especially in fall or spring, is the safest time to use ester formulations. They should not be used if temperatures are running above 90° F; wait until it is cooler or choose another herbicide formulation.

Do Not Spray if Breezy or Windy

During windy or breezy conditions, or when a fine spray stream or mist is used, herbicide particles can drift onto desirable plants, killing or seriously injuring them.

Spray When the Air Is Calm

To prevent herbicide particles from drifting onto nearby desirable plants and injuring them, spray only when the air is perfectly still and use a coarse, narrow spray stream.

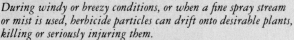

Top: Most herbicides will injure desirable plants if allowed to come into contact with their foliage or stems. This rose leaf shows herbicide injury due to spray drift.
Bottom: When you suspect accidental herbicide damage, be sure to get an accurate diagnosis. The symptoms on this rose leaf are due to a virus infection.

Be especially careful around sensitive plants listed on the label—tomato, rose, and grape, for example—and avoid spraying ester formulations within 6 to 10 feet of them.

SAFETY PRECAUTIONS

Once more: Read the label. It will specify any hazards to be avoided, such as breathing the product or getting it into your eyes or on your skin. These are additional reasons to delay spraying until air is quiet. The label will tell you whether you should wear protective clothing while mixing or applying the product.

The label will also warn of any environmental hazards to guard against, such as keeping spray out of water where fish might be affected or water that you might use for drinking or cooking. If no such warning appears, you can feel comfortable that it is not needed. It seldom hurts, however, to be a little over-cautious.

Above all, use herbicides and other pesticides with as much respect as you have for driving a car or handling tools. By respecting their potential hazard and acting accordingly, you can sit back and fully enjoy their many advantages.

Herbicide Storage and Disposal

Well-formulated herbicides from reliable manufacturers are designed to remain in a stable condition for at least two to three years, providing they are kept in their original containers in a dry, well-ventilated place and are not subjected to excessive temperatures. Avoid places that may stay extremely hot (110° F or more) or below freezing for appreciable periods of time. Many formulations can withstand freezing, merely requiring a good shaking to return to their original condition, but don't count on it only to find that you have an exception to the rule.

Plan ahead and buy only as much as you think you'll need for the current year, so it won't be necessary to store any over the winter. If possible, keep herbicides in a separate closet or cupboard, preferably one that can be locked and that children and pets can't get into. Any herbicide packages should be stored away from food, and away from seeds, fertilizers, insecticides, fungicides, and other materials that will be used on plants. Inspect the containers occasionally to be sure there are no leaks—for example, from corrosion. Never, never, never put any pesticide in a food or drink container or other unmarked container—this could lead to an accidental poisoning.

Don't store unused diluted herbicide. If you can't use it on another weedy area right away, spray it on an unplanted area. Don't pour it down a drain where it could cause unintentional trouble. The label will explain how to dispose of partially or completely emptied containers. Wrapping the container securely with several layers of newspaper and putting it with other trash after a thorough rinsing is sufficient for most herbicides. Check the label, however, to be sure.

NONCHEMICAL METHODS OF WEED CONTROL

Certain garden techniques and cultural practices can stop weeds dead in their tracks. Good gardeners employ such methods as deep mulching, soil cultivation, and judicious hand-pulling to stomp out weeds. They also know that well-grown lawns can shade out weeds and thickly planted garden beds discourage their appearance. These and many other cultural practices are important weapons in the war against weeds.

As with herbicides, cultural control methods can be separated roughly by their function: those that prevent weeds from ever having a chance to raise their new little tops (preemergent methods) and those that eliminate weeds that are already up and growing (postemergent methods). The choice depends on your particular needs: Are tall weeds outgrowing the squash vines? Grassy weeds ruining the look of the flower garden? Clambering weeds winding up the trunks of trees and shrubs? Broadleaf weeds scattered across the lawn?

This chapter describes the basics of mulching to control weeds—which kinds of mulches work best and when and how to apply them. Choosing the proper weeding tool—and using it correctly—can help prevent or eliminate weed pests. Every gardener needs a few tools designed specifically for weed control. The simplest of these is, of course, the garden hoe but there's a whole toolshed full to choose from. Last but not least, watering, fertilizing, and growing techniques that encourage the garden to grow and snuff out weeds should all be part of a gardener's repertoire.

Many kinds of hoes are available to combat weeds. This type is held parallel to the ground to sever weed roots from their tops.

Ground ivy

Deep mulching, regular hoeing, and even hand-pulling can help deter weeds. Find out which mulches and types of tools will do the best job.

MULCHING

The primary way to prevent weeds from sprouting in garden beds is the technique known as mulching—spreading a protective covering over the soil. Mulching is especially appealing to gardeners because it offers so many advantages. Besides shading out weeds organic mulch keeps the soil cool and moist in hot climates, decays into soil-enriching organic matter, and makes the garden look attractive.

Gardeners can choose from a wide variety of mulching materials with differing characteristics. They may be organic (formerly living material such as wood chips) or inorganic (nonliving material such as plastic or gravel). Each works well in different situations.

Most mulches have to be thick enough to prevent light from reaching the soil-borne seeds and stimulating them to germinate. Organic mulches should be at least 2 inches deep to control annual weeds and preferably 4 to 6 inches deep, especially where perennial weeds are a problem. The mulch will discourage any perennial weeds that have been cut back from trying to fight their way through the thick layer, and it may kill some of them outright.

Woodland Lesson

Anyone walking through a woodland, scuffing through fallen leaves on the ground, has encountered nature's own organic mulch. Those decaying leaves create a thick natural covering that allows only a few of the millions of seeds dropped to the forest floor each year to germinate and grow. The rest are smothered under this covering. Those fallen leaves act as moisture equalizers, cushioning the effect of pounding raindrops, minimizing erosion from runoff, and greatly reducing the rate at which moisture evaporates from the soil. They help protect the soil from extreme heat and cold. They slowly become part of the soil itself as they decay. Their organic matter and mineral nutrients enrich the soil, increasing or replacing what is being absorbed by plant roots.

Recreating a woodland mulch in the garden provides several real advantages. Primary among these is weed suppression. Most seeds require a certain amount of light to germinate, and plants must have even more light if they are to grow. If the blanket of mulch is deep enough, it will shut out so much light that weed seeds in the soil or seeds that fall on top won't easily germinate.

Advantages of Organic Mulch

An organic mulch works for a garden in other ways too. As in a woodland it helps retain moisture—an essential function if roots of desirable plants are to grow vigorously, especially during the stress of long dry spells. Instead of allowing wasteful runoff from storms, mulching helps hold rain as it falls and lets it move slowly down into the soil. That reduces or eliminates the need for irrigation, the extent depending on the soil and weather conditions. At the same time mulch acts as an insulator, helping equalize the soil temperature so roots are not subjected to the stress of wide fluctuations or extremes. This can be especially valuable in midsummer and winter in areas with very high or low temperatures. These benefits may not seem directly related to weed control; however, wherever garden plants thrive, they can compete better with invasive weeds.

The influence of organic mulch on soil structure and thus tilth (cultivation quality) can be as important as the labor-saving weed control aspect. It is easy to overlook the importance of adequate air space in soil that an organic mulch encourages. When such a mulch decays it adds nutrients to the soil, lightens heavy soils so they drain better, and increases the ability of light sandy soils to hold water and fertilizer.

In vegetable gardens leaves, grass clippings, and other soft-tissue materials that break down readily can be turned under in the fall, or they can be left on the surface during the winter to protect the soil from erosion and discourage weeds. Growing a green cover crop like annual ryegrass or legumes during the winter and tilling it in in spring also works well.

More persistent materials like bark, pine needles, wood chips, and buckwheat hulls last longer, and often all they need is freshening with a new layer every couple of years.

The loose and well-aerated layer under a mulch provides an excellent environment for a great many of the beneficial microorganisms that help plant growth. The exception is soil that already tends to stay too wet; in this case a mulch might keep the excess water from evaporating.

Another easily recognized mulching advantage is how attractive a well-chosen material makes the garden look. This can be especially important around shrubs and other ornamental plantings where mowing grass is difficult but bare ground would be unattractive. A fairly smooth dark covering makes an effective foil for

luxuriant foliage, colorful flowers, and healthy vegetables as they develop.

Disadvantages of Organic Mulch

As with nearly everything in this world, certain mulches have a few potential disadvantages. Dry ones like straw or sugarcane bagasse can be a fire hazard. Others—notably manures and hay, straw, and other clippings—may bring with them additional weed seeds. This is especially true of manures because they are concentrated wastes and the animals or fowl that produced them have eaten a wide variety of plants. Be sure any farm manure used is well rotted; the heat of composting should kill most weed seeds.

Another thing to remember when using a mulch is that it may offer a home to some creatures you would rather not have. Where they are common, snails, slugs, earwigs, or other moisture-loving pests will move in since the moisture-retaining quality of mulch is very much to their liking. The shelter and soft soil under some mulches, particularly leaves and similar materials, may also attract tunneling rodents such as mice, shrews, and voles. These can feast on plant roots during the winter, causing disastrous results. The bright side is that there are control measures. Traps and pesticides can control insect and animal pests.

Organic mulch not only keeps weeds down, but it also looks attractive and improves the soil as it breaks down.

Another word of caution: If you add too much fresh organic material, such as grass clippings, wood chips, or new sawdust, the amount of nitrogen in the soil can be temporarily reduced while soil bacteria and other microorganisms hungrily decompose the organic matter. Eventually a balance returns, but the deficiency can affect the health of the mulched plants. Yellowing foliage will warn you if this is happening. Prevent the problem by spreading nitrogen fertilizer over the soil just before applying the mulch. A good rule of thumb is 2 pounds of a complete fertilizer, such as 5-10-5 or 8-8-8, per 100 square feet. The same application afterward will correct yellowing. If the mulch is maintained continually, as it ideally should be, this treatment won't have to be repeated.

Sometimes the temperature-retaining ability of a mulch may be too effective. Fresh mulches that have not been composted can heat up when they begin to decompose; this can damage the stems of nearby plants. The solution is to make sure the mulch doesn't touch the stems.

A mulch's temperature-moderating effect can occasionally be a problem. At the end of the growing season, a mulch may keep soil warm when the air is becoming cold. Normally cold weather signals plants to start the process of hardening off that protects them during the winter. The bottom of the trunk or stem of a woody plant is the critical part; be careful that it is not covered by mulch.

Inorganic Mulches

Inorganic mulches run the gamut from gravel to sheets of plastic. Inorganic materials have the advantage of remaining the same, not decomposing while serving their purpose and not introducing new weed seeds. The other side of this coin is that they cannot provide some of the soil-modifying benefits of organic materials.

MULCH CHOICES

There are more choices among the organic mulches and wider differences among the inorganic ones. Which to use depends on availability and cost, as well as the mulch's advantages and disadvantages including appearance and ease of application. Keep in mind that inorganic mulches do nothing to improve soil tilth or quality.

Leaves and Grass Clippings

Tree leaves and grass clippings are the least expensive organic mulches; they are available for the gathering. Oak leaves make a good mulch because they are firm and don't pack down and become matted as do softer leaves such as maple. Leaves may be hard to keep in place except under low-growing shrubs like azalea, rhododendron, and cotoneaster or under open ground covers like euonymus and hypericum.

With most types of leaves it is better to compost them and apply them the next year as leaf mold. Leaf mold makes an ideal mulch and looks neater than uncomposted leaves, which can make a garden look neglected. Leaf mold improves the quality of any soil and makes a superior additive before planting.

Bark, Wood Chips, and Sawdust

Shredded or chunk bark, often from pine or cedar, is an excellent, good-looking, long-lasting mulch. It is readily available at garden centers in many locations. Fresh wood chips may be available locally at little or no cost from tree care services or utility cleanup crews. Such chips may be fine or coarse, depending on the equipment being used. At different times of the year they may be all wood or a mixture of wood and fresh

leaves. Bark and chips work best where they won't be disturbed by cultivation.

Fallen pine needles make a good mulch under shrubs because they have a fine texture, and they tend to knit together and stay in place well without matting or retaining too much moisture. Although their color tends to become grayish after exposure to sunlight, their resins keep them from decomposing very quickly and they look attractive. Needles of the Southern longleaf pine are produced so profusely that they are gathered and sold in bales.

Where it is available sawdust is appealing because its fine granular texture makes it easy to spread and it looks neat, especially when aged enough to have turned a dark brown. Fresh sawdust is light colored and should be composted or allowed to age a few years; otherwise it can cause a severe nitrogen deficiency in the mulched plants. Moist sawdust stored in huge piles may ferment and sour for lack of oxygen and should not be used as a mulch because it can kill plants. Fermented sawdust can be easily identified by its strong odor.

Peat Moss

Whether in bags or bales, from Canada or Michigan, peat moss is a mulching material commonly found in garden centers and other nursery supply stores. It has many appealing advantages—it is essentially sterile (it contains few or no weed seeds), has a warm brown color, resists further decomposition so that it lasts well, and doesn't require extra fertilizer. Bales are so tightly compacted that you

have to break the lumps as you apply it, but any not used immediately can be kept indefinitely until needed.

A peat moss mulch may blow around a bit in the wind until the mulch settles down, but then it stays in place so well that it may felt or mat together and resist wetting by rain or irrigation. In that case it is imperative to break it up to allow water to get through. This tendency to compact and dry out is the major disadvantage of using peat moss as a mulch.

Sphagnum moss is acidic and thus ideal for use under rhododendron and other acid-requiring plants. For use with plants that need alkaline conditions, add 3 to 5 pounds of horticultural lime per 100 square feet of mulch surface to counteract the acidity.

Salt Hay, Straw, and Crop By-Products

From members of the grass family come salt marsh hay, farm field hay, and straw. Of these salt marsh hay decomposes the most slowly and is the cleanest and easiest to work with. When it is available farm hay may be the most economical but you must remember the weed seeds it will bring to your garden, a factor that can be considerably reduced by composting it before use. Otherwise farm hay should be applied thickly enough to smother its own germinating seedlings as well as those already in the soil. The only

A wood-chip mulch discourages weeds and adds an attractive design element to this Japanese-style garden.

seeds you are likely to acquire with straw are those of the grain—wheat, rye, or barley—that produced the straw. Just don't let a lighted match fall on any of these mulches, or they will quickly be reduced to ashes.

Other crop by-products to consider are ground corncobs, sugarcane bagasse, and the hulls of cocoa beans, buckwheat, peanuts, and other seeds. These are all relatively inert, long lasting, and often inexpensive in areas where they are produced. Buckwheat hulls have the finest texture and look quite handsome in flower gardens. Cocoa bean hulls are a nice dark brown, fine textured, and easy to spread, but their odor won't let you forget chocolate. They may mold if they stay damp for very long.

Peanut hulls are more utilitarian, being rather coarse and light colored. Their open cellular nature prevents them from getting soggy, but wind may move them around. Sugarcane bagasse has long fibers that remain in place. Its light color and coarse texture limit it to utilitarian purposes rather than ornamental ones. The same is true of ground corncobs unless they have been colored to make them more attractive. They make an effective mulch, especially if they have been ground fine.

Newspaper and Carpet

There are other organic materials that can work as mulch after they have served their main purpose. Newspaper (made from pulpwood) and worn-out wool or cotton carpeting make surprisingly good mulch where you want utility and where appearance doesn't matter, such as in a vegetable garden. Lay down several sheets of newsprint or other paper, weighting them with soil or stones so they don't blow away. Shredding the paper first makes it easier to spread.

Carpeting can be cut into tidy strips to fit between rows of vegetables, and you may find it amusing to walk on it again, outdoors. Just be sure it doesn't have a rubber backing that will keep water out. Paper and carpeting will break down fast enough over the growing season so that they can be worked into the soil the following spring.

Plastic

As a mulch, black plastic (polyethylene) film provides excellent weed control in a vegetable garden. It may not be advisable for use with woody plants. Under trees or large woody shrubs in temperate climates, a plastic mulch can cause delayed damage due to lack of moisture. The plastic encourages rooting nearer the sur-

face than usual, subjecting large shrubs and trees to drought or blow-down by high winds.

Black plastic prevents weed seeds from germinating, but if the film covers living perennial weeds, strong ones like nutsedge will attempt to push through. Try to eliminate them ahead of time. Less aggressive perennial weeds are usually killed by the lack of light. Spaces between plastic strips may become weedy;

Top: Black plastic, an inorganic mulch, warms the soil under these early-season tomatoes, while ensuring that the bed is weed-free.
Bottom: Fabric mulch lets air and water through, while blocking weed growth. Cover it with bark or pebbles for an attractive garden surface.

cultivate or hoe these areas (see page 32) to keep them free of weeds. Try to avoid walking over the plastic so you don't punch holes that weeds can grow through.

Clear plastic, which lets light through, won't control weeds except in climates where sunlight generates high enough temperatures underneath the plastic to actually cook whatever is there. This is known as soil tarping or soil solarization and is a special technique. In other areas clear plastic can act as a greenhouse and actually encourage rampant weed growth beneath it.

Landscape Fabric

Newcomers to the arsenal of weed controls are polyester landscape fabrics or geotextiles—rolls of thick, feltlike material with pores that allow water to seep through to plant roots below. Landscape fabrics are expensive but they smother weeds, often even nutsedge, and don't rob desirable plants of moisture.

Spread the fabric down on a new bed and cut holes for planting trees, shrubs, and annual flowers. (Landscape fabrics aren't recommended for perennials and ground covers that multiply and spread.) In an established shrub border lay down the mulch, cutting slits and then holes to fit around the existing trunks and stems. To dress up the appearance of the fabric mulch and also to protect it from ultraviolet light, cover it with wood chips or other organic mulch.

Despite the expense, the durability and adaptability of landscape fabric may be worth the cost in areas to be kept mulched indefinitely. It will last and keep out weeds for many years. However, during this time an organic mulch covering may begin to decompose and provide a medium for germinating weed seeds. If this happens remove and replace the organic mulch.

Stones

Crushed stone, chips, gravel, or pebbles appeal to some gardeners because they come in a variety of colors, shapes, and sizes, but they don't control weeds well unless a layer of plastic (punctured to allow water through) or fabric mulch is first put on the soil. This technique works best for ornamentals in low-rainfall and desert areas. The mulched plants don't suffer from lack of moisture and the stones are in keeping with the natural landscape. Stones may get very, very hot in sunshine and stress the plants. On the other hand, stones don't absorb pest-attracting moisture.

CHOOSING A MULCH

Which mulch to choose depends primarily upon the garden site. For a flower garden or planting of woody ornamentals, appearance is probably the most important factor. Peat moss, leaf mold, seed hulls, or finely ground or shredded bark work well and look attractive. The mulch can be thin enough in a flower bed so that it can be worked into the soil and replaced annually. On the other hand, shallow-rooted woody plants—especially azalea, mountain laurel, blueberry, and others in the rhododendron family—grow best when a thick mulch of leaves, wood chips, pine needles, or bark covers the soil at all times.

Small stone chips work well with sun-loving rock-garden plants or cacti. Buckwheat hulls seem right for rose gardens. There they needn't be dug under for two or three years, although replacement or renewal each spring may help discourage soil-borne diseases like blackspot. For wildflowers nothing seems more appropriate than leaves or leaf mold. For more information about mulching in flower beds, see pages 42 and 43.

In vegetable gardens coarser materials such as straw, hay, ground corncobs, or peanut hulls, can be used. The choice depends on what is available and economical. Several heat-loving vegetables, especially tomato, pepper, eggplant, sweet corn, and cucurbits (cucumber, squash, and melon) seem to benefit from black plastic. For more information about mulching in vegetable gardens, see pages 40 and 41.

DON'T PICK UP HITCHHIKERS

Because new patches of weeds can start from only a small piece of a readily rooting perennial weed—for example, slender speedwell, Canada thistle, or quackgrass—be sure to keep cultivators and lawnmower clean. It may be a great convenience to hire a neighborhood kid to mow the lawn, but check that the mower blades are cleaned between lawns—speedwell, for instance, has been known to hitchhike on mower blades from one lawn to the next.

As a safeguard against freeloading weeds, when buying plants look closely at their rootballs to see whether an invasive weed shares the soil. Chrysanthemum weed, which infests many woody plant nurseries, is infamous for piggybacking into gardens, where it rapidly becomes one of the most persistent of weeds. Quackgrass, Canada thistle, and nutsedge often travel this way too.

Beware of nursery plants bearing noxious weeds. The oak tree in this container is accompanied by nutsedge.

Federal certification requires lawn and other seeds to be nearly pure. All seeds must be inspected and every package must carry a list of what is in it, including any weed seeds. Read the label carefully, especially when considering inexpensive seeds for a lawn area because some of these are not produced as meticulously. Rarely are quality commercial seeds a source of contamination.

Finally if you decide you need topsoil be sure it's clean. Remember the cunning ways weeds can survive while hidden underground as pieces of root or dormant seeds, bulblets, or tubers.

SOIL CULTIVATION

If you have inherited weeds but were unable to control them last year or let a new crop get started this year, there are still many ways to control or eliminate them without herbicides. The most familiar way, of course, is traditional cultivation with a hoe. It's important to begin cultivating as soon as tiny weeds appear, starting as soon as possible in the gardening year so the weeds don't get a head start. They will only grow larger and greedier as the season advances.

Chopping off seedlings while they are young and tender, with only two to four leaves, can stop them before they have a chance to develop their means of survival. This prevents reproductive roots, crown shoots, or seeds from forming to start a new batch of weeds. It is easier to control annual weeds than established perennial weeds by hoeing. However, even with perennials winning is possible by keeping at it systematically.

The thing to remember is that weed leaves are the factories that convert the energy of sunlight into sugars that fuel plant growth. When their tops are removed, they have to use stored energy to produce new tops. If you're clever enough and determined enough to cultivate the soil regularly, eventually the weed's stored energy is exhausted and it perishes. Sometimes when the weed grows too close to desirable plants or too thick to dig out or spray, this battle of attrition is the only way to win. It requires patience and constant persistence.

Never letting weeds produce seeds is a basic key to control in the long run. For the same reason try to keep weeds in nearby wild areas from forming seeds that could invade your garden.

Proper Technique

Cultivating needn't be the backbreaking chore it is sometimes reputed to be. To avoid disturbing the roots of desirable plants, cultivate shallowly, shaving weeds off just below the soil surface. This technique avoids bringing more weed seeds (remember, there are probably thousands of them buried underneath) up to an unmulched surface where they can get enough light, air, and moisture to germinate. Shallow cultivating also breaks up soil crusting so that water can penetrate more easily. To keep the cultivation shallow, hold the blade of the hoe almost parallel to the ground.

Limit cultivating to when it is clearly needed and where it is needed. If done too often and too thoroughly, cultivating can break down soil structure and lead to compaction. That's another thing that mulching helps avoid and a strong argument in its favor.

Tools for Cultivating

Several types of tools make good cultivators. Each works best under different conditions. The size and type of garden site to be cultivated also influence the choice of tool.

Use a rake—square-back or bow but not a flexible leaf rake—to get new beds ready for planting. Rake through the top of the soil, pulling out pieces of roots or stems and even whole weed plants as you level the soil. Raking eliminates a good many weeds right at the start.

For larger areas there are more complex tools ranging from wheel cultivators to powered ones; rototillers and disks and drag hooks pulled by tractors are useful in dealing with areas so large that they approach a commercial scale.

Cultivators are great for stirring soil and uprooting some weeds, but for controlling weeds a hoe works better. A hoe enables you to cut weeds off near the surface without going deeper and without cutting the roots of desirable plants. The blade of a scuffle hoe moves a little as it is pushed or pulled, changing the cutting angle and cutting weeds off better than a fixed-angle hoe.

Since a hoe is essentially a cutting tool, it works most easily if kept sharp—sharpen it as often as after every couple of hours of use, especially in stony soil. To sharpen, file the blade at a 45-degree angle, then smooth the back by rubbing the file across it flat to take off any burs.

After planting choose a short-handled cultivator or fork for fine work in small spaces between plants. One of the most useful has tines made of spring steel. It is very flexible so you can merely scratch the surface or dig down under the root mass of an established weed. Long-handled versions are tools like potato hooks that can be maneuvered where there isn't much room. An asparagus cutter or other knife is great for cutting under a single weed. It may be necessary to go back and cut deeper with a spade.

Weeding is least difficult if the soil is moist, so do it soon after a rain but when the soil is no longer muddy or sticky. Remember, working wet soil can compact it by squeezing the air out and jamming soil particles together. If it's too dry sprinkling the soil with water ahead of time helps.

Opposite: Many types of tools aid in the fight against weeds. Some can chop up seedling weeds, others slice mature weeds off at the soil surface, and still others dig out a weed, roots and all.

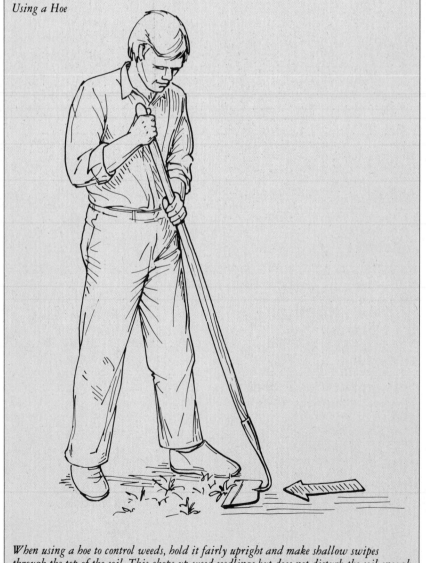

Using a Hoe

When using a hoe to control weeds, hold it fairly upright and make shallow swipes through the top of the soil. This chops up weed seedlings but does not disturb the soil enough to bring up more seeds to the soil surface where they can germinate.

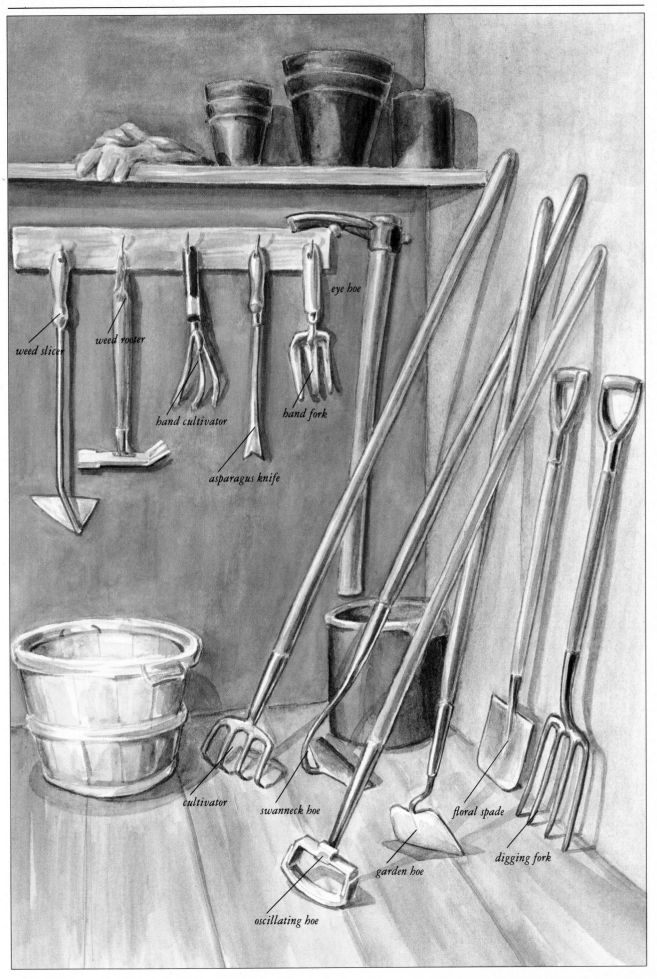

weed slicer

weed rooter

hand cultivator

asparagus knife

eye hoe

hand fork

cultivator

swanneck hoe

oscillating hoe

garden hoe

floral spade

digging fork

Top: *A hand cultivator can quickly uproot weed seedlings growing between desirable garden plants.*
Bottom: *In very small areas and under vegetable crops, hand-pulling can be an effective method of weed control. When the soil is moist, pull one weed at a time to be sure the entire root comes out.*

Except in rainy weather most of the weeds that are cut will die if just left on the surface. However, there are a few that will try to keep right on growing. Purslane is one of these and it should be raked off and thrown on the compost pile. (You can clean it, cook it, and enjoy it as a potherb if you prefer.) Beware of perennial root parts that might keep growing or of thistles and related plant structures that often continue developing seeds after flowering stems have been cut. Throw them on the compost heap, where the heat of decomposition will eliminate their hazard.

MOWING

Where it isn't desirable or practical to attempt controlling weeds by cultivation, mowing is effective too. It interrupts the growth of the weeds, forcing them to use reserved food for renewal. Mowing often delays or eliminates flowering and thus seed set for that year. To reduce future problems be sure to mow before the weeds set seed. Mowing a meadow or other place intended for grasses or wildflowers also holds reforestation at bay by nipping off tree seedlings and keeping them at mowing height instead of letting them grow into giants. Mowing can also keep climbers, such as Japanese honeysuckle, down on the ground where they can form a rather nice cover if there is room. Mowing is a great help in suppressing multiflora roses whose hips are scattered so generously by birds.

Tall weeds can choke a lawn mower. Go at them with a scythe or spinning monofilament weed whip. These whack back weeds in open areas and in otherwise inaccessible spots, such as around poles, tree trunks, or walls. Don't let the whip hit trees and shrubs, however. It can skin or bruise the bark, especially if the bark is young and thin. When using this tool, follow the manufacturer's safety instructions, which usually advise wearing goggles. The weed whip can easily flip up a small stone or other bit of debris and cause serious eye injury.

HAND-WEEDING

If all else fails you can still pull weeds by hand, laborious as that may seem. Actually, hand-weeding can be a rather pleasant way to tend the garden. Being so near to your plants helps you become more aware of their condition and habits. When hand-pulling weeds don't throw them on the ground. This can spread seeds or roots of weeds that have been removed, so consign them to the compost heap.

Since most garden weeds are annuals, they are shallow rooted and pulling them out is simple. Loosen the clump before pulling and you're most likely to get the whole weed instead of merely breaking off the top. It also helps to break off roots all around and twist the entire weed before pulling slowly. Parts left behind—especially if there's a bit of crown or root with buds on it—can keep growing and produce more tops.

KNOW YOUR WEEDS

While going about the business of weeding by hand or with a tool, it will help your success rate to get acquainted with the way each weed grows and especially with its root structure. Some, like carpetweed, are easy to eliminate because they have roots only at the very center of the plant. Plantains are this way and so are dandelions; the entire taproot must be pulled out or it will resprout.

Other weeds send out shoots that root wherever they touch the ground. That's how ground ivy and nimblewill are able to form such large patches. You soon come to realize that every sprig of these ramblers must be removed or otherwise destroyed if you're going to get rid of them. Their roots are shallow so it's relatively easy to clear them out. However, the roots of some other weeds may go very deep, indeed, and spread out too. That's what make Canada thistle and quackgrass such formidable adversaries. You may think you've gotten rid of them when you cut off their tops, but buds on those deep roots are lurking underground waiting for the signal to start growth. When the tops of mature wild garlic plants are pulled out, hidden bulblets are left behind. Although the crisp foliage tufts of nutsedge seem to come away easily, they leave behind a network of roots with tiny daughter tubers at their tips ready to keep growing after the mother shoot has been removed.

Regardless of which weeding method you choose, be sure not to leave behind parts that can regenerate and nullify your effort. If you've missed a few, go back and eliminate those before they have a chance to multiply.

TEND YOUR GARDEN

Even desirable garden plants can join the fight against weeds if given ammunition in the form of proper fertilizer and water.

Tend your garden regularly so plants become vigorous and able to compete successfully with weeds. This is especially true in lawns. When the turf is not well cared for or is under stress from heat and drought, crabgrass and broadleaf weeds invade and outcompete the grass.

Close Planting

Intensive gardening, a technique in which vegetables and flowers are planted close together rather than in well-spaced rows, can deter many weeds by shading them out. Space the transplants or seedlings so that the foliage of neighboring plants, when mature, will touch or mingle slightly.

Such closely spaced plants may need extra water and fertilizer. Weeds may be a problem while the garden is young, but a little hoeing will deter them until the garden plants take over.

When weeding, the watchwords are "get 'em young and get 'em early"—before they have a chance to become unattractive pests and before they have a chance to use water and nutrients intended for your plantings. The sooner weeds are eliminated, the more time you will have to enjoy your gardening as you envision it in your dreams.

A well-tended garden with vigorous, closely spaced plants is able to compete with weeds and shade most of them out.

SELECTING THE RIGHT CONTROL METHODS

Sheep sorrel

Not all weed control techniques are equal. Some work better in vegetable gardens and others work better in lawns. This chapter describes how to choose among the different weed control techniques discussed in the first three chapters to effectively battle weeds in different garden areas around the home.

CONTROLLING LAWN WEEDS

Although lawns are often thought of as needing a good deal of care, they actually require less effort than many other living ground covers.

Lawns are communities of tightly crowded plants that have insufficient room to develop fully. Unlike most other plants, grasses grow from the base, which makes it possible to clip them constantly. Mowing allows you to have a pleasing, compact, and permanent live cover, but cutting off the tops reduces the food-producing factories that these plants need in order to survive and grow. The added competition of greedy weeds can make the going even tougher.

Eliminating weeds from lawns is quite easy with the proper herbicide application. Preemergent applications (see page 19) control certain annual weeds; postemergent applications (see page 19) control lawn weeds once they are visible. Homeowners can apply these treatments themselves or hire a professional lawn care service.

Doing it yourself has several advantages; you can apply the herbicide at the best time without waiting your turn on

Applying mulch over weed-free soil under flowers prevents new weeds from germinating and beautifies the flower bed.

Controlling weeds in vegetable gardens requires a different plan of attack than does combating them in a lawn. Learn which herbicide, mulch, or weeding technique works best for each lawn and garden area.

a schedule that includes many other clients. You can choose the kind of weed control and monitor the quality and accuracy of its application. It's usually less expensive, even after investing in application equipment. You can apply granular herbicides with a lawn spreader and liquid ones with a hose-end sprayer (see pages 21 and 22).

On the other hand, reputable professionals (check credentials before signing any agreement) are skillful and

knowledgeable. Their experience comes from extensive training and daily experiences under many conditions. Good ones know which safety precautions to take, and they may use effective herbicides not generally available to home gardeners.

Being able to identify the weeds you intend to control and understanding the way they grow are essential to success. The Encyclopedia of Weeds beginning on page 47 details the most common lawn weeds and includes the names of the herbicides that work best on each type of weed.

Keep in mind the kind of turfgrass—or if it is a mix, the kinds of turfgrasses—in the lawn. The major types are either cool-season or warm-season grasses. Cool-season grasses, which remain green throughout the year but grow best when weather is cool, include bluegrass, fescue, and bentgrass. Warm-season grasses grow actively during late spring, summer, and early fall but are dormant and brown from midfall until midspring. They include bahiagrass, bermudagrass, centipedegrass, St. Augustine grass, and zoysiagrass. When they are actively growing, warm-season grasses may be injured by some broadleaf herbicides. Some of these herbicides, however, won't harm the grass if it is dormant.

Preemergent Control

The major warm-season turfgrasses generally tolerate the preemergent herbicides available to homeowners: benefin, benefin plus trifluralin, bensulide, DCPA (Dacthal®), siduron, and pendamethalin. DCPA gives consistently good results under a variety of conditions, although bermudagrass may be injured by siduron. Among the cool-season grasses, fine fescue and bentgrass tend to be somewhat

A good way to apply a selective herbicide to a lawn is with a broadcast applicator such as a hose-end sprayer. Be sure to use the sprayer only for lawn treatments or for applying herbicides.

sensitive to benefin with or without trifluralin and to DCPA. Instructions appear on the labels for use on sensitive grasses.

The price of a treatment of benefin may cost less than one of the others, but it does not last as long and another application may be required to assure control for the rest of the summer.

All the preemergent herbicides just mentioned kill by interfering with the germinating seed. Apply them in late winter or early spring, as recommended on the label, before the expected germination time so that the herbicide can get into the soil where seedling roots can absorb it. If weeds have already started to emerge, it will be too late to affect any seeds except late-germinating stragglers or summer flushes. For information about preemergent treatment of crabgrass, see page 56 of the weed encyclopedia.

Although you can't count on it controlling seedlings that have already emerged, a good preemergent herbicide will remain effective for 60 to 90 days or even longer, depending on soil and weather conditions. This is especially important in combatting a weed like crabgrass whose seeds don't all germinate at the same time. A too-light irrigation or rain after a dry spell can trigger the germination of more seeds throughout the summer unless prevented with a suitable preemergent treatment.

With proper treatment you can expect 80 to 90 percent control of annual grasses and broadleaf weeds for three to four months. Rain or irrigation following the treatment works to your advantage by washing the active ingredients in more thoroughly. Control is not always 100 percent so pull or cut out any weeds that escape control.

Most preemergent herbicides shouldn't be used when reseeding a lawn because they will kill the desirable grass seedlings as well as the weeds. After a spring application enough of the herbicide will be gone by midsummer so you can reseed then if need be. It is better, however, to wait until fall because that is a better time to plant a lawn. If you must control annual grasses like crabgrass and reseed very soon afterward, choose siduron for a cool-season lawn. Siduron has a shorter period of effectiveness than other preemergent products—only about a month, but it can be applied at any stage of lawn development including immediately after seeding. It controls crabgrass in the one- to three-leaf stage, something the other herbicides don't do. DCPA (Dacthal®) can also be applied after new cool-season lawn seeds have emerged, but no sooner.

Postemergent Control

Selective postemergent treatment is practical for eliminating most annual and perennial broadleaf weeds from your lawn. The phenoxy group of herbicides (2,4-D, MCPA, MCPP or mecoprop, and 2,4-DP or dichlorprop, used separately or combined) and dicamba are by far the most widely used. They have recently been joined by triclopyr, a phenoxy relative that was first used for controlling woody plants. Each phenoxy herbicide controls a slightly different range of weeds, making multipurpose combination formulations very sensible since they control a wide range of weeds with a single application. They allow you to operate on a shotgun theory: If one doesn't quite do the job, another of the components is likely to. There are very few weeds that don't respond to one of the components or to a combination.

Most grasses tolerate selective broadleaf herbicides without being injured—that's the beauty of selectivity. As with preemergent herbicides, a few grasses are a little sensitive (bentgrass, bahiagrass, centipedegrass, St. Augustine grass, and some varieties of hybrid bermudagrass). Label directions advise using a half-rate application for these and applying the other half about a week later. An alternative is to choose a formulation of just MCPP, which these grasses tolerate a little better.

It will be necessary to repeat the treatment if the lawn is infested with persistent perennial weeds—for example, field bindweed or Canada thistle—that can regrow from bits of root the herbicide didn't reach. New seedlings, especially of spurge, oxalis, and a few other summer annuals, may germinate after you apply herbicide. Control them with another treatment later on as directed by the product label. Bromoxynil is the one herbicide that can be used selectively to control broadleaf weeds emerging in newly seeded turf. Delay applying any of the others until newly seeded turfgrass has become established well enough to be mowed two or three times.

If you miss the time for preemergent treatment of crabgrass, postemergent treatment is not quite as simple. It requires enough selectivity to kill the weedy kind of grass growing with a desirable kind. Organic methanearsonates have been used for many years for this purpose, and they may be combined with 2,4-D to control broadleaf weeds at the same time. Methanearsonates (which do not contain arsenic) don't actually kill the sprayed plant; they prevent new growth and consequently few or no new seeds will develop. Usually at least two treatments about two weeks apart are needed for control.

Crabgrass, dallisgrass, foxtail, and other annual weedy grasses respond best while they are only 1 or 2 inches tall and not yet crabbing out. Turfgrasses are usually more resistant to injury then too. Although postemergent treatment may turn many turfgrasses yellow, the discolored blades disappear in two or three weeks with mowing. Watering and fertilizing after treatment help the grass turn green more quickly. Avoid treating when grasses are under stress, as during drought or extreme heat.

Reliable as herbicides are, when you plan to erase broadleaf weeds from your lawn with a selective product, be sure to reread the sections in the second chapter about selective herbicides, how they work, and how they should be applied.

Spot Treatment

A few patches of crabgrass, nutgrass, foxtail, barnyardgrass, goosegrass, and dallisgrass in a lawn can be spot-sprayed with methanearsonate without harming the turf. There is no selective herbicide for weedy perennial grasses like orchardgrass, quackgrass, nimblewill, tall fescue, common bermudagrass, or bentgrass. Carefully spot-treat scattered clumps or patches of these grasses with a nonselective herbicide such as glyphosate. If bare spots from their removal are too large for turf to quickly fill in, reseed or resod a week later after removing the dead grass. The only other option is to cut the weeds out manually, being sure to remove any crown or root parts from which they might regrow.

Crowd Out Lawn Weeds

The best weed deterrent is a thick, healthy lawn. Mowing, fertilizing, and watering properly are the keys, assuming the turfgrass is adapted to the climate and growing conditions. Assuring proper drainage, avoiding excessive wear, and controlling any damaging insects and diseases help in the fight against weeds too.

Good lawn care practices are as important as killing existing weeds. Mow regularly, removing only about a third of the leaf surface each time. Close-clipped lawns look neat, but it is much better to let cool-season grasses grow a little taller. Setting the blades at a height of 2 to 3 inches helps protect roots from summer heat and provides enough shading to discourage germination and growth of

many annual weed species. The reverse is true with most warm-season turfgrasses. They grow strongly during the summer and, except for bahiagrass and St. Augustine grass, need close clipping to keep them tight to the ground where it is hard for weeds to invade.

Top: This pronged weeder, often called an asparagus knife, is designed for removing individual deep-rooted weeds from lawns. Bottom: Lawn grasses mowed to their optimum height fight weeds best. Set the mower to cut grass to the optimum height for the variety.

Weedy lawns are generally malnourished. A soil analysis will indicate which nutrients are needed. Most states offer this service at little or no cost, and it's the smart way of maintaining proper lawn fertility. Find out about this service through the cooperative extension office in your county or through the state university. Short of having a soil analysis, a general rule of thumb is to apply 3 pounds of actual nitrogen per thousand square feet of lawn every year. Do not apply more than 1 pound per thousand square feet in a single application unless the nitrogen is in slow-release form or you risk burning the grass. Choose a fertilizer like 10-6-4 that contains a higher percentage of nitrogen than phosphorus or potassium. The first number in a fertilizer formula always stands for nitrogen, the second number phosphorus, and the third number potassium. For cool-season lawns, apply the fertilizer in September when the grass is beginning its most active period of root development. Apply another part of the total in November for maximum winter hardiness, and an additional low-rate touch-up in mid- to late spring. If you live in an area where it is necessary to water the lawn because of a lack of rainfall, apply a slow-release nitrogen fertilizer in early summer.

In contrast to cool-season grasses, to do their best warm-season grasses need to be fed each month while they are green and growing actively. Stop fertilizing in late summer to slow grass growth and thus prevent frost damage to tender new growth.

Except for centipedegrass, turfgrasses grow better and for a longer period if the soil pH (measure of acidity) is nearly neutral or around 7.0, permitting best use of fertilizer elements. To raise the pH of acid soil to the neutral point, apply horticultural lime. In alkaline soil apply soil sulfur, ammonium sulfate, or iron sulfate to lower the pH to the neutral point. A soil test is the only satisfactory way of estimating the amount of amendment needed. These amendments can be applied any time of year but late fall is usually best.

In most arid regions, especially in California and the Southwest, lawns must have constant irrigation if grass is to remain green through the summer. In most areas, however, watering should be an all-or-nothing matter: Water deep or not at all. Frequent shallow watering is worse than none, weakening turf and encouraging the growth of many weeds, especially crabgrass. Slowly soak the soil several inches deep when the grass wilts enough

Using Lawn Herbicides

These simple tips help assure success in using herbicides for lawns.
☐ Remove fallen leaves and other debris before treating the lawn.
☐ Apply the product as directed on the label.
☐ If the lawn is dry, water it the day before applying the herbicide.
☐ Water the lawn after applying a pre-emergent to help move the chemical into the soil where it can do its job.
☐ Select a dry period with no rain forecast when applying a postemergent herbicide.
☐ Apply a postemergent herbicide when weeds are actively growing.
☐ Apply a preemergent herbicide just before weed seeds begin to germinate.

to curl and footprints remain. If you start watering you must continue, repeating only when the wilting stage has been reached again.

Lawn Renovation

If a lawn is so thin and weedy that you think the only solution is to dig it up and start over, think again carefully. Digging up a lawn does let you add organic matter and fertilizer to the soil, but it also brings to the surface more weed seeds to continue the weedy condition. Fixing the problem usually means changing cultural practices. Check the factors just discussed to see which might be causing poor lawn growth and try to take corrective action.

Most problem lawns are suffering from malnutrition. Regular fertilization can often improve lawns. For thin weedy lawns use a single application of a product containing a broadleaf herbicide and a fertilizer.

If a lawn has more weeds than turfgrass, renovation may be the answer. Don't dig up the lawn, but kill everything growing in it with an herbicide. Glyphosate is excellent for the purpose. Nonselective, it will start to kill the weeds and grasses right away and is inactivated in the soil almost as quickly. Apply the recommended amounts of fertilizer and amendment to adjust the pH level and sow seeds right over the dead turf and weeds a week later. Treated vegetation can be mowed and left where it is, acting as a mulch that protects the germinating grass. For cool-season grasses, such renovation is best performed in fall when cooler weather arrives. Renovate warm-season grasses in spring when plenty of moisture is available.

CONTROLLING WEEDS IN VEGETABLE GARDENS

Because there usually is open ground between the plants in a vegetable garden, eliminating and preventing weeds there often seems like a never-ending chore. Weeding can be held to a minimum by following some basic principles.

Fight Weeds in Fall

In the fall after the last vegetables are harvested, begin a preventive routine. Cut down on the number of next year's weeds by killing any that are still growing. A few persistent weeds may yet set seed and perennial weeds are still storing energy in their roots, absorbing additional nutrients from the soil while they do it. Get rid of them. Cultivate thoroughly with a hoe, pull weeds out by the entire root, or spot-treat them with an herbicide listed for use in a vegetable garden. Controlling weeds in the fall means they won't come back to haunt you the next spring. In warm-winter areas where vegetable gardens can continue through the winter, follow the same weed-fighting techniques as you do during the rest of the year. Effectiveness of herbicides may be limited by temperatures, however; check the label before applying in cool weather.

In cold-winter climates, plowing or deep cultivating in the fall can deplete the soil of weed seeds. It brings weed seeds to the surface where they begin to germinate but are killed during the winter. Fall is also a time to consider fumigating with metham (Vapam®; see page 19). In warm-winter areas early fall is a good time to apply a preemergent herbicide to prevent spring weeds (see page 19).

Fight Weeds in Spring

Till the soil and add organic matter well before you intend to plant vegetable seeds or set out transplants. Shallow cultivation or rototilling early in spring helps too. Then hack down weed seedlings with a hoe before planting, taking care not to disturb the soil enough to bring more weed seeds to the surface. Every weed killed and its offspring prevented from forming before vegetables are planted is one less weed to worry about later.

Mulching

Mulching vegetables provides numerous advantages besides smothering weeds (see page 28). Straw, hay, grass clippings, leaves, paper, sawdust, ground corncobs,

Top: Organic mulch protected this vegetable garden from weeds when the plants were small. Now the crops have filled in so well that sprouting weeds don't stand a chance.

Bottom: A thick organic mulch keeps weeds from competing with vegetables. Straw is an economical and effective choice for a vegetable garden.

and locally available organic mulches are usually economical. Be sure that the mulch is free of weed seeds, that you apply it thick enough (3 to 4 inches) to smother annual or biennial weed seedlings, and that you first make a light application of nitrogen fertilizer (see page 28).

Black polyethylene film is the most practical of the synthetic mulches for vegetable gardens. It comes in rolls 3 or 6 feet wide and can be laid down and unrolled over the rows where you intend to sow seeds or set out transplants. Black plastic doesn't add organic matter to the soil, but it does keep it loose and moist so beneficial microorganisms thrive. In areas where there isn't year-round vegetable gardening, the plastic may last 3 or 4 years if it is taken up in the fall and put back in place in spring. It isn't necessary to mulch the entire area—just the rows where it is so hard to eliminate weeds. When cultivating an unmulched space between the rows, be careful not to tear the plastic.

After laying down the plastic, use a knife to make slits through which to set young transplants or insert seeds. If covering more than a few square feet of surface, punch small holes with a spading fork or other sharp tool to help water penetrate; soaker hoses or drip irrigation tubes can also be positioned beneath large sheets of plastic. Be sure to weight the edges of the plastic with rocks or bury the edge of the sheet so the wind doesn't blow it off.

plantings of many different kinds of vegetables and some of these may be injured by the treatment. A few compounds could remain in the soil and harm crops planted there the next year. Application of those registered for home use must be carefully controlled to avoid injuring sensitive plants by unintended herbicide movement (drift or leaching).

Postemergent herbicides are not approved for broadcast or spot application among home garden vegetables during the growing season. Two preemergent herbicides can be used on clean-cultivated soil to control certain annual weeds but only where the garden will be planted with any of the vegetables listed on the label. Granular DCPA (Dacthal®) and trifluralin can be used this way with many vegetables, especially those in the cabbage family. Before using either of these herbicides, *read the label carefully* to be sure which crops and weeds are listed and what precautions are necessary.

CONTROLLING WEEDS IN FLOWER BEDS

Most of the information for controlling weeds in vegetable gardens also applies to flower beds. Light cultivation, hand-weeding, and mulching are the three most practical ways of controlling weeds in these areas.

Mulching

An organic mulch, with its attendant advantages (see page 28), is the best way to reduce the hours needed to control weeds. At the same time it dresses up the garden and prevents soil from splashing onto the foliage and blossoms. Remember, however, to fertilize under organic mulches. Finely ground bark, buckwheat or cocoa bean hulls, ground corncobs, and colored sawdust are among the most attractive mulches and are easy to handle. Grass clippings can be used alone or mixed with peat moss, sawdust, or ground corncobs to prevent their packing down. Just be sure not to use grass clippings from lawns that have been treated with an herbicide within the previous two weeks. Should sawdust form a crust as it dries, you can quickly break that up by a very light raking with a potato hook or other small cultivator that

Cultivating

Regular shallow cultivation is the time-honored alternative to mulching for weed control in vegetable gardens. Cultivate before planting to clear away any existing weeds and resume as soon as new weed seedlings start to emerge. Keep it up regularly so they don't have a chance to get ahead in competing for nutrients, water, and space. With a small garden the easiest way is to shave weeds off with a hoe when they only have a few leaves and well before they flower. Keep the hoe sharp and your strokes shallow so you don't injure roots or bring up a fresh supply of weed seeds. With large gardens choose a wheel cultivator or a rototiller, but keep the cultivation shallow when using either implement to control weeds.

In harvesting sections of the garden, do not leave the soil bare if it is unmulched. Replant with a new crop, following a warm-season vegetable with a cool-season crop if the climate permits. An alternative is to work up the soil and plant a green manure of ryegrass or soybeans to suppress weeds and to add organic matter when you turn them under.

Deep-rooted perennial weeds—quackgrass, bindweed, Canada thistle, nutsedge, and a few others—are the most troublesome because they come through most mulches and resprout after cultivation. Constantly removing their tops to ground level and cultivating to cut the roots (particularly in fall so they are exposed to winterkill) may eliminate some, but it is hard to get rid of those capable of regenerating from small pieces of root left behind.

Using Herbicides

Herbicides are a boon in controlling persistent perennial weeds in vegetable gardens. Long before planting time you can fumigate with metham (Vapam®; see page 19) or you could have used a systemic herbicide as a spot cleanup treatment the previous fall. Glyphosate works well then and is ideal to use this way after the last harvest, if applied according to label directions around listed vegetables.

Several selective herbicides are available for use on commercial vegetable crops where large fields of a single kind of crop are grown. Few of these are practical—or registered for use—for home gardens. Home gardens contain small fits between the plants. Although peat moss looks attractive, you will find its tendency to mat is a problem because it sheds water and is hard to break up.

Black plastic film, so useful in vegetable gardens, won't work well in flower beds because placement of the flowers is closer and more irregular than with vegetables. Plastic sheeting doesn't allow perennials to multiply and spread.

Cultivating

As with vegetables cultivate flower gardens shallowly so you don't damage roots of desirable plants. Cultivate frequently so that weeds never get very big, much less flower and set seed. A 4-inch-wide potato hook or spring steel Magic Weeder® work especially well. The latter is available with a 5-inch handle for getting close to your work or a longer one that allows you to stand up while working. With little open space between flowers, hoes aren't quite as useful as in vegetable gardens because there's always a chance that roots of the flowering plants will be cut.

Hand-Weeding

Removing weeds when they're young is the key to success when hand-pulling them. Many people prefer to hand-weed, finding it immensely satisfying to get right in there with the plants and soil. Results are immediately visible. Try to see just where the roots are coming from, then give the weed a slight twist as you pull it out—or tease it out slowly so you get as many of the roots as possible and don't damage roots of adjacent flower plants. Hand-weeding works best when the soil is moist.

Using Herbicides

The same preemergent herbicides available for use on vegetables—DCPA (Dacthal®) and trifluralin—provide excellent weed prevention in flower beds. These prevent the appearance of grasses and broadleaf weeds in flower beds and are especially useful in controlling annual weeds, which are prolific seeders. Neither herbicide will control annual or perennial weeds that are already established. Apply these herbicides in spring to weed-free soil. DCPA control lasts six or eight weeks and breaks down fairly fast in warm, moist soils so it doesn't leave a harmful residue. You can use it just before transplanting but after transplanting is better. Around seeded flowers wait until seedlings are at least 3 inches tall. These herbicides can be used with nu-

Grassy weeds can be easily controlled in a flower bed by using a selective herbicide in a ready-to-use trigger applicator.

merous annual and perennial flowering plants; consult the labels for which ones.

Weedy annual grasses growing in flower beds can be controlled by postemergence application of fluazifop-butyl applied over many species of flowering plants as listed on the product label. These include coleus, gazania, geranium, marigold, petunia, zinnia, several perennials, and woody ornamental plants.

By exercising great care you can use glyphosate for spot treatment of weeds growing in flower beds. Make absolutely sure this nonselective herbicide does not get on any other plants, because it will kill them too. (You can shield desirable plants from the spray as described on page 24.) The value of glyphosate is that it eradicates most deep-rooted perennial weeds that can't be controlled otherwise.

Among the chemical helpers available for use in flower beds, fumigating with metham (Vapam®) can be useful in the fall if you are planning a brand-new bed for spring (see page 19).

CONTROLLING WEEDS IN GROUND COVERS

A new planting of ground covers, such as myrtle, pachysandra, or English ivy, has a lot of open space that invites invading weeds. Until the plants become established enough to shade out weeds, you will have to battle the invaders. A thick organic mulch may prevent many weeds from appearing but should not be deeper than 2 inches or the ground cover may have difficulty spreading.

You can consider fumigating the fall before planting (see page 19), but it is simpler to encourage weed seeds in the top ½ inch of soil to germinate by light watering and then to kill them by cultivating. This procedure will eliminate a large part of the weed problem before you plant.

A preemergent herbicide does a somewhat more thorough job of eliminating newly germinating weeds, especially grasses, from the soil surface. Trifluralin is registered for use on several ground covers including ajuga, ivy, hypericum, ice plant, and sedum. It should keep the ground clear of weeds for four to six months while the ground cover plants become established and start to provide their own weed control by shading. DCPA (Dacthal®) is one of the safest herbicides to use on ground covers. The list of ground covers on which it is approved for use includes several species of ivy, juniper, lantana, pachysandra, and sedum. You can count on its control lasting at least two to three months.

Where grasses poke through ground covers that haven't spread out enough yet, you can use fluazifop-butyl over a number of broadleaf ground covers: ajuga, several species of ivy, dichondra, lily turf, hypericum, pachysandra, periwinkle (myrtle), and juniper.

Deep-rooted perennial broadleaf weeds may be the very worst problem in new or established ground covers. Eliminating them with carefully applied spot treatments of glyphosate may be the only satisfactory answer even though you may damage a little ground cover in the process. It is almost impossible to dig out such pests as Canada thistle, field bindweed, quackgrass, and mugwort (wild chrysanthemum) once they become established. Again prevention is the best cure, so try from the very start to keep weeds from developing.

CONTROLLING WEEDS AROUND SHRUBS AND TREES

Keeping the ground free of weeds under plantings of ornamental shrubs and trees is easier than in flower gardens, because the woody plants are not as fragile as herbaceous annuals or perennials.

Mulching

Organic mulches, such as bark, wood chips, leaf mold, or pine needles, look decorative and keep weeds down. Using them avoids root damage that might result from cultivating. Keep in mind the basics of applying the material deep enough (3 to 4 inches) to be effective. Scatter a little nitrogen fertilizer over the soil surface first, although this may not be as important as with closely planted, shallow-rooted flowers. Once in place mulch should last for several years but can be renewed each year with another inch or so of material.

If one or more of those old bugaboos—field bindweed, Canada thistle, nutsedge, or bermudagrass—pushes through, it's a signal to consider a less open mulch; one of the new landscape fabrics that lets water through freely while suppressing weeds is a good choice (see page 31). Adding a covering of organic mulch camouflages the fabric so it looks better.

Herbicides

DCPA (Dacthal®) and trifluralin, which can be used in flower and vegetable beds, prevents grasses and broadleaf weeds from appearing beneath certain shrubbery listed on the product labels. A third herbicide, dichlobenil, controls a wide range of mostly annual grassy and broadleaf weeds around many established woody ornamentals. It must be incorporated or watered in thoroughly soon after application, preferably in late fall or winter when temperatures remain below 50° F, because it is volatile. Cold rain or snow after application is ideal. Be especially careful to keep the application uniform so you don't overdose or underdose; don't apply it on slopes because granules or impregnated soil could wash off and injure turf or other plants on the down side.

Glyphosate is useful for spot treatment of stubborn weeds under shrubs

A mulch of landscape fabric keeps most weeds from growing beneath shrubbery for years, and it allows air and water to reach the shrub roots. Concealing the fabric beneath a thin layer of bark mulch blends it naturally into the landscape and protects the fabric mulch from ultraviolet light.

Top left: Herbicides let you control poison oak (shown here) or poison ivy without having to touch the irritating plants. The foam marker in this product identifies treated plants.
Top right: This herbicide product kills existing weeds and prevents more from sprouting for months. After a three-month waiting period, small rock garden plants can be planted in the weed-free soil.
Bottom: To control tree root suckers, dig down and find their point of attachment to the tree root. Then cut them at the root, using a sharp knife.

and trees. It is usually more effective on maturing weeds than younger weeds early in the growing season. Use it to eliminate weeds before planting ornamentals or around established plantings. Take caution not to spray the foliage or stems of the shrubs and trees; mature corky bark won't absorb glyphosate, but thin green bark can absorb it resulting in serious injury to the shrub.

Weed Whips

Power tools with a spinning filament or blade, often called a weed whip, are being used more and more to cut back weeds growing around and right next to tree trunks. They are handy but watch closely to be sure you don't cut shrub or young tree bark at the same time. Girdling or seriously injuring stems can result in dead tops. The filament may seem innocuous but don't let that lull you into carelessness.

CONTROLLING WEEDS IN WALKS AND PATIOS

Gravel driveways, brick or stone patios, clay game courts, pathways, and curbs look best when kept clear of all vegetation. A few of the toughest weeds seem to thrive in cracks in these surfaces and are difficult and annoying to hand-pull.

Using Herbicides

Glyphosate kills existing weeds in these areas, but one of its biggest virtues—that of being inactivated in the soil—is a disadvantage in such situations. It has no residual action to control any weeds that emerge after the treatment. By combining glyphosate with another herbicide that has residual action for the rest of the growing season, existing and future weeds can be controlled. Products containing a combination of glyphosate and oxyfluorfen work well.

Prometon is a powerful herbicide that kills existing vegetation and prevents new

growth for about a year. When using this material take special precautions to prevent runoff. Avoid spraying too close to trees and shrubs because their roots could absorb this semisterilant. Do not spray soil that contains tree roots. Remember, roots usually extend many feet beyond the drip line of the tree's branches. Don't spray prometon on sloping ground where it might move downhill with runoff water. As when using any herbicide, be sure to *read the label* and follow directions exactly.

CONTROLLING BRUSH

When weedy woody trees, shrubs, and vines overgrow an area or need to be cleared out, cutting them down usually isn't enough. Most will resprout from stumps or roots left in the ground. A combination of physical removal and herbicide treatment usually works best.

You can spray the foliage of the entire plant and let the herbicide travel through the plant to eventually kill it. This requires a large amount of herbicide and you may have difficulty preventing it from drifting onto desirable nearby plants. Of course, the dead branches will remain. An alternative is to cut the offending tree or brush to the ground and immediately treat the stub with an herbicide so that it doesn't resprout. You can use the same kinds of materials used for broadleaf weed control in lawns but labeled with appropriate directions for brush control. Choose triclopyr or 2,4-D and apply it undiluted to the cut stump. Reapplication may be needed for complete control. A contact herbicide can be applied to suckers sprouting from tree roots to control the unwanted growth, or the suckers can be cut off below ground where they join the root.

ENCYCLOPEDIA OF WEEDS

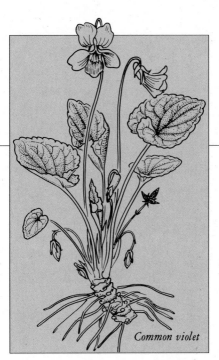

Common violet

Described and pictured here are over one hundred weeds commonly found throughout the United States in lawns, flower and vegetable gardens, under shrubs, and twining around trees. Some favor sites where little else will grow—and where you would prefer nothing to grow anyway—such as between the bricks of a patio or walk, in a gravel driveway, and even on a tennis court. Here you'll learn how to identify and control the particular weeds that trouble your lawn and garden.

Identifying and Naming Weeds

The weeds are presented in alphabetical order by their most well known common name. Almost every weed has several names by which it is known, and many of these names are included in the listing. Some names may refer to more than one plant—a cause for confusion if using common names only. That's why the weed's botanical name is listed as well. A botanical name refers to one and only one plant and is used universally.

To easily locate the entry for a weed that you know only by an alternate common name, look up that name in the index; it will refer you to the proper page. If you don't know the name of the weed, browse through the encyclopedia looking at the pictures and reading the descriptions of likely candidates.

If a weed doesn't look quite like any of the ones illustrated or referred to in this encyclopedia, it may be for one of two reasons. Although some specimens of a weed look essentially like all the other ones of that species, some develop with minor differences and may not look exactly like the one pictured.

Familiar as an old shoe, common weeds such as dandelion and clover dot many a lawn.

Here is a rogues' gallery of common lawn and garden weeds. There is a mug shot of each weed to aid in its identification, and the text describes how to best combat the weed.

The other reason you may not be able to match your weed is that it may not be included here. If this is the case, a local garden center may have someone on staff who can identify the weed, or your county's cooperative extension service can help. Send a representative sample including seed head or flower, stem, leaves, and underground parts. Forward it in a sealed plastic bag or foil wrap without moistening and it will arrive in fresh enough condition to be readily identified. This is especially important when sending grasses, which are difficult to identify. You can also press the weed between the pages of a telephone book.

Using the Encyclopedia

The beginning of each encyclopedia entry discusses what makes the weed a problem and how it thwarts gardening goals. Does it increase so aggressively that it threatens to populate a whole area? If it goes to seed in the garden, will it be a problem for years to come? Will it smother desirable plants or merely coexist with them, looking messy but doing little real harm?

The section called The Weed provides a physical description of the weed and its life cycle. Read this section carefully for clues to a weed's identification. It may include descriptions of related weeds or comparisons with weeds that it resembles.

The section called Control Measures is a guide to combatting the weed. Both chemical and cultural control methods are given where they are effective. Because different techniques and herbicides are suitable for different garden locations, these are presented under separate headings. Refer to the earlier chapters in the book for detailed instructions on particular techniques.

When a herbicide is suggested, its common (generic) name is given. Such names appear on herbicide product labels in the list of active ingredients. Check the labels of any herbicides that you are considering buying to see if the chemical is listed. The name of any Ortho product that contains that active ingredient, lists the weed to be controlled, and is registered for use in the garden area under question is given in parenthesis after the common name of the suggested herbicide. In some instances, where a manufacturer's brand name is more commonly known than the common name, it is also included. Not all products are sold nationwide; some may be available only in certain geographical areas.

ANNUAL BLUEGRASS

Poa annua
(Annual spear-grass, dwarf spear-grass, walk-grass)

The white, tufted seed heads of annual bluegrass look unsightly in lawns. When this annual weed dies out in summer, it leaves behind bare spots that may be mistaken for disease. It prefers fertile soil but can tolerate low nitrogen and compaction. The weed is highly variable; some types persist as perennials, especially in cool climates.

The Weed
This little grass seldom grows taller than 4 to 8 inches in lawns or a bit more in open ground. Like other bluegrasses, its leaf blades have a transparent line on each side of the midrib. The bright green leaves are sometimes crinkled at the middle and their tips turn up like the prow of a boat. Roots are shallow and fibrous. Stems sometimes bend and root at

Annual bluegrass is so similar to many lawn grasses that it may not be obvious in the lawn until it forms seeds and dies back, turning yellow.

the base, but this weed does not form rhizomes. Flowers appear profusely in mild climates, beginning in midwinter.

Abundant seeds produced during most of the growing season germinate in late summer, early fall, or spring, given cool weather and adequate soil moisture. Usually a winter annual, bluegrass is very susceptible to heat injury.

Control Measures
In lawns: Excellent pre-emergent control can be obtained with benefin, bensulide, or DCPA (Dacthal®—Ortho Garden Weed Preventer) applied in late summer or early fall. Improve general turf quality (including aerating for better drainage) if needed.

In gardens: Cultivate and mulch clean soil, or cultivate and then apply benefin, bensulide, or DCPA (Dacthal®—Ortho Garden Weed Preventer). Use trifluralin around listed flowers and vegetables. Fluazifop-butyl (Ortho Grass-B-Gon® Grass Killer) can be used selectively for postemergent control over and around many flowering plants.

Around woody ornamentals: Control as in gardens, and you may also spot-treat with glyphosate (Ortho Kleenup® Grass & Weed Killer), or apply dichlobenil (Ortho Casoron® Granules) to clean, level ground.

BARNYARD-GRASS

Echinochloa crus-galli
(Cockspurgrass, watergrass, summer grass, cocksfoot panicum)

This weedy grass competes vigorously with desirable plants in all garden areas. It appears mostly in thin, newly seeded or wet areas. Growth becomes flat when mowed, but the weed continues to thrive and form seeds.

The Weed
Although appearance varies, barnyardgrass can be distinguished from other weedy grasses by the complete absence of a ligule (membrane

Barnyardgrass is an annual grass that makes a pest of itself in every part of the garden, especially in wet, poorly drained spots.

where the leaf sheath and blade join) and by its coarse, chunky flowering shoot, which has a central stem with several spreading branchlets and short, stiff hairs.

It has fibrous, rather shallow roots. The weed reproduces only by seeds that are dormant for several weeks after they mature but can germinate from early spring to early fall. The seedling stems are purplish. Most seedlings emerge from the top ½ to 1½ inches of soil. Maximum emergence is in spring, decreasing as the season advances but often continuing until a killing frost. It develops fastest from seeds germinating in late spring or early summer. Late-emerging barnyardgrass is shorter but fuller. The weed is most noticeable in late summer and early fall.

Control Measures
In lawns: Prevent the weed with a preemergent application of benefin, bensulide, or DCPA (Dacthal®—Ortho Garden Weed Preventer). Encourage thicker turf with good management.

In gardens: Eliminate emerging seedlings easily with continuous shallow cultivation. To minimize further appearance of weeds, maintain a mulch after clean cultivation or apply bensulide, DCPA (Dacthal®—Ortho Garden Weed Preventer), or trifluralin around listed flowers or vegetables.

Around woody ornamentals: Control as in flower gardens. Dichlobenil (Ortho Casoron® Granules) may be applied to clean, level ground.

BERMUDAGRASS

Cynodon dactylon
(Wiregrass, devilgrass, scutchgrass, dogtooth grass, vinegrass, couchgrass)

Widely used as turf in the South, bermudagrass is also one of the most invasive and defiant of weeds. Bermudagrass is either the primary lawn grass or the primary lawn weed in many parts of the United States. Only heavy shade discourages it. Brown and dead-looking in the winter landscape, it comes back to life in spring with renewed vigor. This weed is spreading northward and is aggressive where it survives winterkill.

The Weed
This creeping perennial has 1- to 4-inch-long, fine-textured, flat leaves with a distinguishing tuft of white hairs at the base of the blades. Its stolons (aboveground creeping stems) are scaly and somewhat flattened, and they bear at each joint a dead, bladeless sheath resembling a dog's tooth. The rhizome (rootstock) is hard, scaly, and sharp enough to pierce the root mass of other plants.

Although it makes a good lawn in hot climates, bermudagrass has the bad habit of spreading to other parts of the garden, where its roots and runners are difficult to remove.

Upright flowering stems develop into slender dusty umbrellas with 3 to 9 finger-like spokes above the foliage. Reproduction is primarily by rapidly spreading rhizomes and stolons that produce aerial shoots or new plants as they root at nodes.

Control Measures

In lawns: There is no selective control. Use repeated spot treatment with glyphosate (Ortho Kleenup® Systemic Weed & Grass Killer) in fall or fluazifop-butyl (Ortho Grass-B-Gon® Grass Killer) in early spring as the weed turns green. Then reseed.

In gardens: Fumigate large infested areas before planting. Cultivate intensively; roots and rhizomes are killed by exposure to the sun. Hand-pull, being careful to remove as much rootstock as possible, or spot-treat with glyphosate (Ortho Kleenup® Systemic Weed & Grass Killer). Apply fluazifop-butyl (Ortho Grass-B-Gon® Grass Killer) around listed trees, shrubs, and ground covers.

Around woody ornamentals: Control by spot-treating with glyphosate (Ortho Kleenup® Grass & Weed Killer) before or after planting or apply fluazifop-butyl (Ortho Grass-B-Gon® Grass Killer) around listed trees, shrubs, and ground covers. Mulching will do little to control this persistent weed.

BINDWEED, FIELD AND HEDGE

Convolvulus arvensis and *Calystegia sepium* (Wild morningglory, cornbind, creeping-jenny, creeping-charlie, greenvine, European bindweed)

These viny, weak-stemmed, persistent perennial weeds are one of the most troublesome and successful competitors for moisture and plant nutrients. They invade fields, gardens, and lawns, especially in regions with little rain, and develop extensive root systems, overwhelming nearby plants.

Field bindweed's cordlike main roots commonly go down 8 to 10 feet; depths of 20 to 30 feet have been recorded. So many buds on the horizontal roots develop new shoots that an undisturbed plant can form a patch 20 feet across in three years. Small pieces of root left behind in the soil after hand-pulling or cultivation can easily start new patches. Buried seeds have remained alive for at least 30 years, waiting for the right conditions to start growing.

The Weed

Stems of field bindweed are slender and curl on the ground or twine up any nearby support, soon blanketing it. Bluntly arrow-shaped leaves vary in size but are relatively small with rounded tips and almost straight bases. White or pinkish flowers that look like nickle-sized morningglories last only one day but form seeds constantly from early summer until frost. The seeds are almost indestructible.

Hedge bindweed, which actually belongs to a different genus, has much larger flowers and leaves than field bindweed. Its leaves are triangular with pointed tips, and bases that are more deeply cut. Despite their relative shallowness, the roots are extensive. The weed reproduces by sending up new plants from buds on the severed roots. Hedge bindweed also reproduces by releasing large quantities of seed. Its pretty flowers appear from late spring until early fall.

Control Measures

In lawns: Control is difficult. The best response is from products with 2,4-D (Ortho Weed-B-Gon® Jet Weeder–Formula II) or 2,4-D combined with dicamba (Ortho Chickweed, Spurge & Oxalis Killer D) repeated every two weeks, according to label directions, each time new shoots appear. Complete control may take several years. Supplying adequate moisture and otherwise thickening turf will also help.

In gardens: No method of control is easy or works completely. Any treatment may take several consecutive seasons for effective control.

Occasional cultivation may spread bindweed instead of reducing the population. Keep all tops cut to prevent production of new seeds. Constant cultivation from spring until frost may keep bindweed down but not out. Where plantings permit, repeated spot sprayings with 2,4-D or glyphosate (Ortho Kleenup® Systemic Weed & Grass Killer) reduce infestations, but extreme care must be taken to avoid killing nearby plants at the same time. See product labels for limited permissible use with vegetables.

If the infestation is severe enough, consider a year or two without plantings so you can deeply cultivate the area (to a depth of 4 inches) every two or three weeks from spring until fall to eliminate growth from roots. Another option is to allow some foliage to develop for spray absorption, then treat with 2,4-D in late summer or early fall while the bindweed is still growing actively. Then cultivate intensively the following spring.

Around woody ornamentals: Spot-treating with glyphosate combined with acifluorfen (Ortho Kleenup® Grass & Weed Killer) provides excellent control. Repeat the treatment whenever new shoots appear. Then apply a thick organic mulch or a landscape fabric mulch to discourage shoot growth.

Whether it is carpeting the ground or climbing garden plants, field bindweed is one of the most noxious of weeds.

BISHOPS GOUTWEED

Aegopodium podagraria
(Goutweed)

Because it spreads so enthusiastically, goutweed is used as an ornamental ground cover where its vigor is an advantage. If it escapes to where it isn't wanted, it can be a persistent weed. Goutweed grows in full sun but prefers moist shade and can blanket the edges of a woodland or other planting it invades. (A variegated form with white leaf margins is somewhat less aggressive.)

The Weed

Toothed compound leaves, similar to those of celery, arise from rhizomes at the ground surface. The upright flowering stems bear umbels (rounded clusters) of tiny white flowers

Be careful where you plant bishops goutweed. Although attractive as a ground cover, it can be very difficult to eradicate if it escapes.

in summer. Goutweed reproduces by seeds and new shoots from branching rhizome networks that spread wide and deep, propagating dense weed patches.

Control Measures

In lawns: This weed is resistant to 2,4-D. Constant mowing will eventually exhaust root reserves.

In gardens and around woody ornamentals: Trying to dig out goutweed is futile. Spot-treating with glyphosate (Ortho Kleenup® Systemic Weed & Grass Killer) is worth a try.

BLACK MEDIC

Medicago lupulina
(Black clover, trefoil, hop medick, yellow clover)

Usually a summer annual weed, black medic can behave like a winter annual, a biennial, or occasionally like a perennial. Black medic forms spreading patches in lawns and smothers the turfgrass in thin, infertile lawns.

The Weed

Its wiry stems come from a shallow but tough taproot and are usually downy, especially at the base. Stems lying on the ground may be a couple of feet long; upright ones are shorter. The tripartite leaves, which resemble clover, have shallow-toothed tips, with the center leaflets growing on short stalks. Small, nearly round clusters of little yellow flowers appear on stalks above the leaves. The ridged, one-seeded pods become black and kidney-shaped or slightly coiled when mature. Black medic blooms from early spring to late

Cloverlike leaves, yellow pea-type flowers, and black kidney-shaped or slightly spiraled seedpods identify black medic.

autumn, sometimes into December, and drops seeds most of that time.

Control Measures

In lawns: Black medic doesn't respond to preemergent treatments of available lawn herbicides. Spray existing weeds with a product containing 2,4-D, dicamba, or MCPP alone or in combination (Ortho Chickweed & Clover Control, Ortho Chickweed, Spurge & Oxalis Killer, or Ortho Weed-B-Gon® for Southern Lawns). Thicken turf with good management practices to crowd out black medic.

Clover Comparison

Two clovers, black medic (top) and white clover (bottom), are often confused when they occur as lawn weeds. The rounded black medic leaflets have points at the tips, and the leaflets of white clover are uniformly rounded. Flowers of black medic are yellow and those of white clover are white or pinkish.

In gardens: This weed is hard to hand-pull, but it can be done if the ground is moist. However, frequent cultivation is more effective. Mulch to suppress new seedlings.

Around woody ornamentals: Clear the soil with a sharp hoe, then mulch. Spot-treat with glyphosate (Ortho Kleenup® Grass & Weed Killer). Dichlobenil (Ortho Casoron® Granules) provides excellent pre-emergent control.

BULL THISTLE

Cirsium vulgare, syn. *C. lanceolatum*
(Common thistle, spear thistle)

Although often confused with Canada thistle (see page 52), a major problem weed, bull thistle is a relatively minor one in spite of its fearsome, needle-pointed spines on leaves and stems. It can be aggressive in fields but does not successfully invade lawns or survive in cultivated gardens.

The Weed

Bull thistle is a biennial. Its first year is spent as a solitary, ground-hugging rosette of prickly, coarsely-toothed leaves which can easily be seen and removed. Not until the second year does it develop a deeper taproot and send up a woody, flowering stalk. Only a few of the large, handsome, rose-purple

Since bull thistle is a biennial, you will have the entire first season to notice and eliminate its ground-hugging rosette of thorny leaves before the plant forms a flowering stalk.

blooms appear on each stalk. (Canada thistle produces many small flowers from early to late summer or early fall.) The plumed seeds of bull thistle are fertile (unlike most of the seeds of Canada thistle) and are its sole way of reproducing.

Control Measures
Wherever seen: As soon as the weed is recognized, cut off below the rosette or spot-spray with glyphosate (Ortho Kleenup® Systemic Weed & Grass Killer) to prevent seed production. In lawns use 2,4-D combined with dicamba (Ortho Chickweed, Spurge & Oxalis Killer D) to kill emerging rosettes.

BURCLOVER, CALIFORNIA

Medicago polymorpha,
syn. *M. hispida*
(Toothed burclover, medic)

This cloverlike weed is useful for forage in pastures, but it infests lawns and landscaped areas as well as cultivated commercial crops. An annual unable to withstand summer heat, burclover also lacks winter hardiness and grows only in mild, moist regions.

The Weed
Its smooth stems may trail on the ground for 2 or 3 feet. Tips are usually upright and bear slender-stalked clusters of two to five or more tiny yellow flowers characteristic of the clover family to which it belongs. Burclover can be distinguished from black medic (page 50), which it resembles, by the toothed margins and indented tips on the three-leaflet leaves. The unique seedpods, tightly coiled, have a double row of soft spines (burs) along the edge.

Spotted or southern burclover (*M. arabica*) is a perennial with little purplish markings on its leaves.

Control Measures
In lawns: Use a postemergent herbicide containing MCPP combined with dicamba (Ortho Chickweed & Clover Control, Ortho Chickweed Spurge & Oxalis Killer D). Check cultural practices to keep turf thick.

In gardens and around woody ornamentals: Cultivate

Burclover spreads by barbed seedpods that attach to clothing and animal fur. A close inspection of the seedpods reveals that they are pea-type pods, twisted into a spiral.

early to eliminate seedlings and prevent flowering and seed formation. Maintain a good mulch to discourage burclover from germinating in winter. Spot-treat with glyphosate (Ortho Kleenup® Systemic Weed & Grass Killer).

Woolly white leaf undersides help to distinguish rosettes of burdock leaves from those of other weeds.

BURDOCK, COMMON

Arctium minus
(Clotbur, wild rhubarb, cuckoo-buttons)

BURDOCK, GREAT

A. lappa

Widespread, but not serious pests, burdocks can grow from 2 to 5 feet tall. They prefer rich soil. Annoying, bristly flower heads cling to clothing, hair, or even each other, enabling the seeds to be scattered.

The Weed
These biennial cousins have large heart-shaped leaves that are smooth on top. They are woolly underneath—unlike those of cultivated rhubarb, a plant that burdock resembles. They form dense rosettes the first year and send up flowering stalks the second year if allowed to grow that long. The flower heads, covered with purplish hooked bristles, break off easily when dry and brown at maturity.

Control Measures
Wherever found: Cut the large, deep taproot just below the basal leaves the first year to prevent flower and seed formation the next year. Spray with 2,4-D alone or combined with MCPP (Ortho Weed-B-Gon® Lawn Weed Killer) or dicamba (Ortho Chickweed Spurge & Oxalis Killer D); or spot-treat with glyphosate (Ortho Kleenup® Systemic Grass & Weed Killer).

BUTTERCUP

Ranunculus species
(Crowfoot)

Several species of buttercup have crept into lawns and occasionally gardens from meadows or fields where they are more common. Most are easily recognized by the shiny golden flowers and glossy leaves which are usually deeply divided. The plant is not related to Bermuda buttercup, which is not a *Ranunculus* but an *Oxalis* or woodsorrel (see page 91).

The Weed
All weed species—whether summer annual, winter annual, biennial, or perennial, reproduce by seed. Buttercup flowers range from minuscule to almost an inch across. Most have fibrous roots, although bulbous buttercup (*R. bulbosus*) has a short, thick bulblike base by which it can reproduce, and creeping buttercup (*R. repens*) is a perennial that spreads by rooting at nodes.

Control Measures
In lawns: Spray a postemergent herbicide containing MCPP, 2,4-D, or dicamba (Ortho Chickweed, Spurge & Oxalis Killer D, Ortho Weed-B-Gon® Lawn Weed Killer). Mow to prevent flower and seed formation.

In gardens: Eliminate by cultivating and preventing new seeds.

Bulbous buttercup reproduces not only by seeds, but also by a thickened bulblike base that sends up new plants.

Around woody ornamentals: Shallow cultivation or mulch—or both—are usually sufficient. Dichlobenil (Ortho Casoron® Granules) effectively prevents seed germination.

CANADA THISTLE

Cirsium arvense
(Creeping thistle, small-flowered thistle, perennial thistle)

Not actually a native of Canada, this thistle is now found there and throughout the northern half of the United States. It has been declared legally noxious by 37 states because of its greedy invasiveness. Canada thistle is a tough perennial that forms dense

An underground view of Canada thistle would explain why the weed is so difficult to eliminate: Its massive root system extends 10 feet deep and sends up many shoots.

patches of prickly foliage from its wide-spreading root system. Roots reach as deep as 10 feet and spread horizontally into a large system capable of sending up new shoots every foot or less. A whole colony in an open

area actually may be a single plant that spread as its roots extended and sent up additional shoots.

The Weed
The oblong leaves are more or less lobed, usually with crinkled edges and spiny-toothed margins. Numerous small lavender to rose-purple or white flower heads are borne in compact clusters on 1- to 5-foot-tall stems that branch near the top. Sexes are borne separately on different plants. Both fertile and sterile seeds are formed and float about on breezes. Seed production can be as high as

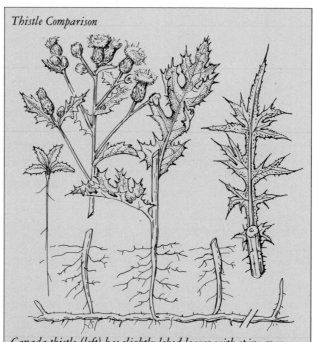

Canada thistle (left) has slightly lobed leaves with spiny margins. Its flower stalks contain numerous small flowers. Leaves of bull thistle (right) are deeply lobed and contain spines on all surfaces, including the stems. Bull thistle flowers are larger and less numerous than those of Canada thistle.

5,000 per female plant, so don't let this weed go to seed.

Tops tend to die back after flowering, but there is a new flush of growth in early fall that may continue to be active as late as November.

Distinct types may vary in leaf shape and degree of spininess, flower color, height, or response to herbicides.

Control Measures
In lawns: Whatever method is chosen must be repeated. Keeping tops and rosettes constantly mowed eventually discourages their reappearance. Treat with 2,4-D (Ortho Weed-B-Gon® Lawn Weed Killer). Better control may be achieved with 2,4-D combined with dicamba (Ortho Chickweed, Spurge & Oxalis Killer D) or combined with triclopyr—but the treatment can still take up to three years.

In gardens and around woody ornamentals: Keep Canada thistle stalks cut to prevent seed production. Herbicide treatment is most effective at the bud-to-bloom stage, but it may be more

practical to keep the tops constantly hand-pulled or hoed. Where possible, spot-treat rosettes of leaves as they form, using glyphosate (Ortho Kleenup® Systemic Weed & Grass Killer, Ortho Kleenup® Grass & Weed Killer). Since small severed pieces of root can start new plant colonies unless they are destroyed at once, cultivating can present a problem and so is not recommended.

CAROLINA GERANIUM

Geranium carolinianum
(Carolina cranesbill, wild geranium)

This native weed is common throughout the United States in disturbed soils, especially poor, dry ones. It rarely causes a serious problem, but its presence in lawns and shrub borders is unsightly. Generally a winter annual, Carolina geranium may develop as a biennial.

The Weed
The usually five-parted, deeply cut, hairy leaves are particularly conspicuous against the brown of dormant, warm-season turfgrasses. The leaves may become reddish as they die back. Clusters of small pale pink or white flowers with notched petals appear in spring and develop prominent beaked seedpods about ½ inch long resembling cranes' bills. Seeds, its means of reproducing, are scattered by a violent upward snap of the elastic outer walls of the mature seedpod.

Control Measures
In lawns: Carolina geranium is readily controlled by applying 2,4-D alone or with dicamba (Ortho Weed-B-Gon® Lawn Weed Killer, Ortho Chickweed, Spurge & Oxalis Killer D). Improve soil conditions by proper fertilization, watering, and liming if needed.

Carolina geranium, a small-flowered native geranium, may become a pest in lawns or gardens.

In gardens and around woody ornamentals: Eliminate Carolina geranium by cultivating in spring and again in late fall if seedlings appear. Fertilize adequately and water when needed.

CARPETWEED

Mollugo verticillata
(Indian-chickweed, whorled chickweed, devilsgrip)

An inoffensive summer annual that grows rapidly after getting a late start, carpetweed soon covers bare soil with flat circular mats.

The Weed
Pointed, strap-shaped leaves are whorled around spokes of smooth green stems. Branching in all directions from a shallow taproot, carpetweed does not root at the nodes as do many more aggressive weeds. From early summer until fall, clusters of pale green or white flowers bloom on slender stalks emerging from whorls of five or more leaves at each node.

Control Measures
In lawns: Preemergent application of DCPA (Dacthal®—Ortho Garden Weed Preventer) for crabgrass control minimizes emergence of carpetweed too. Fertilize in fall or early spring and correct any other factors that limit development of vigorous turf.

In gardens and around woody ornamentals: Carpetweed is easy to eliminate by hand-pulling. Prevent emergence of the weed by applying DCPA (Dacthal®—Ortho Garden Weed Preventer) or trifluralin, or maintain a mulch applied before seedlings emerge. Use shallow cultivation to eliminate established weeds and prevent formation of more seeds.

Carpetweed branches until it forms a mat of stems around the central rooting site. It has a taproot that is easy to hand-pull.

CHICKWEED, COMMON

Stellaria media
(Starweed, satin flower, starwort)

Troublesome throughout the world, common chickweed is a delicate looking but tough winter annual. The floppy growth roots at nodes, and although its fibrous roots are shallow, chickweed forms smothering blankets as it matures. Familiar in vegetable and flower gardens, chickweed is also one of the most common weeds in lawns, where its presence indicates the grass is thin.

Chickweed often alternates with crabgrass. As temperatures rise, chickweed dies out. The resultant bare spots are quickly invaded by crabgrass, which then dies out in the fall and is succeeded by more chickweed as cool weather returns.

Two other familiar chickweeds, mouseear chickweed (*Cerastium vulgatum*) and the closely related little starwort (*Stellaria graminea*), are perennials. They have slender leaves and behave quite differently (see mouseear chickweed on page 54).

The Weed
The tender, bright green leaves of common chickweed are smooth and almost heart-shaped. Stems have a curious band of hairs that switch sides above and below each node. Starry white flowers that appear by midwinter or very early spring seem to have 10 petals, but these are really 5 deeply cut ones. Common chickweed blooms and sets seed throughout its growing season. Seeds begin to germinate early in the fall and continue throughout the fall, or later in mild climates.

Control Measures
In lawns: Eliminate common chickweed with an herbicide containing MCPP (Ortho Chickweed & Clover Control), or MCPP and dicamba (Ortho Chickweed, Spurge & Oxalis Killer D), or MCPP and 2,4-D (Ortho Weed-B-Gon® Lawn Weed Killer) preferably when the weeds are still small. A preemergent

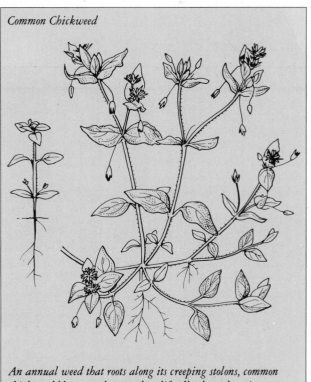

Common Chickweed

An annual weed that roots along its creeping stolons, common chickweed blooms and sets seed prolifically throughout its growing season. Even seedlings (left) have flowers.

In cool seasons a vegetable garden, flower bed, or thin areas of a lawn can disappear under a mantle of chickweed.

application in fall of benefin, bensulide, or DCPA (Dacthal®—Ortho Garden Weed Preventer) provides some control. Keep chickweed out by developing thick turf with adequate soil fertilization, liming if needed, mowing at the proper frequency and height, and judicious watering.

In gardens and around woody ornamentals: Remove weeds by frequent shallow cultivation or mulching, or control with DCPA (Dacthal®—Ortho Garden Weed Preventer) or trifluralin applied to weed-free soil.

CHICKWEED, MOUSEEAR

Cerastium vulgatum

This weed's common name fits it so well that it has no other. Usually a vigorous perennial, mouseear chickweed grows almost anywhere. It becomes established in open places in gardens and in lawns where turf is light as well as where it is thick. The weed spreads by horizontal stems that root where the nodes touch the soil, forming small patches of dense growth that crowd out desirable plants. Flowering and seed set of this perennial continue from late spring until frost.

The Weed
Closely resembling common chickweed (see page 53), mouseear chickweed actually belongs to a different genus.

Slender horizontal stems grow from fibrous, branched, shallow roots that are nearly transparent. Pairs of oblong, stalkless leaves are almost as softly hairy as the ears of mice, distinguishing it from common chickweed. Groups of about three small white flowers with five notched petals are borne at the ends of bare stems and produce numerous rough seeds that are long-lived in the soil.

Control Measures
In lawns: This weed competes aggressively with healthy turf, and is therefore hard to control. Spray patches with an herbicide containing MCPP (Ortho Weed-B-Gon® Lawn Weed Killer, Ortho Chickweed & Clover Control) or dicamba (Ortho Chickweed, Spurge & Oxalis Killer D)

Small leaves with soft hairs earned this weed the common name mouseear chickweed.

in late summer or early fall for best results. A preemergent application of DCPA (Dacthal®—Ortho Garden Weed Preventer) will prevent mouseear chickweed.

In gardens and around woody ornamentals: This weed does not persist when the soil is cultivated. Remove small patches by hand or spot-treat with glyphosate (Ortho Kleenup® Systemic Weed & Grass Killer, Ortho Kleenup® Spot Weed & Grass Killer). Around woody ornamentals kill established weeds and prevent germination with glyphosate plus oxyfluorfen (Ortho Kleenup® Super Edger). Apply dichlobenil (Ortho Casoron® Granules) as a preemergent in late fall or winter in beds under shrubs and trees.

CHICORY

Cichorium intybus
(Succory, blue sailors, blue daisy, coffeeweed, blue dandelion)

A Eurasian perennial that escaped from cultivation, chicory now bedecks vacant lots, roadsides, pastures, and gardens across the United States. Although it can be a pest, especially in lawns, chicory is attractive to look at and has its uses in the kitchen. It is sometimes cultivated for its thick roots, which make a pleasantly bitter-tasting coffee substitute when dried and roasted, and for its leaves, which can be cooked or used in salads.

The Weed
Generally a perennial but occasionally a biennial, chicory forms a rosette of leaves during its first year. The leaves resemble those of dandelions, except they are rough and hairy. Most are long and narrow with irregular indentations around the edges. Numerous flowers appear the second year, blooming from midsummer until late fall. The flowers, which close by midday, are usually a lovely sky blue but may be white, or on

Chicory's flowers, usually sky blue, open in the morning and close in the midday sun.

rare occasion, pink. They appear singly or in clusters along the rigid, almost leafless, stiffly-spreading, 1- to 3-foot branches. Leaves grow mostly at or near the base.

Although most reproduction is by seed, chicory develops a deep, rough, strongly branched taproot from which it can regrow after cultivation. Seeds are peg-shaped with only a row of tiny, bristly scales instead of the plume that dandelion seeds have.

Control Measures
In lawns: Apply 2,4-D (Ortho Weed-B-Gon® Lawn Weed Killer) to rosettes with or without flowering stems.

In gardens and around woody ornamentals: Unless deeply cut, roots may resprout, so hand-weeding is not recommended. Chicory seldom survives repeated deep cultivation.

CINQUEFOIL

Potentilla canadensis and *P. simplex*
(Five-finger, barren strawberry)

These two weedy plants resemble each other closely—they are both perennials with hairy stems that creep on the ground for a foot or more. The stems root at nodes to produce new plantlets and are thus invasive. Cinquefoil usually grows in dry, sandy or gravelly soil that is often acid.

The Weed

Cinquefoil bears leaves with five leaflets arranged like the fingers of a hand. (The common name is derived from the French *cinque* meaning five, and *feuille*, meaning leaf.) These yellow-flowered weeds have five wedge-shaped leaflets that are rounded with teeth above the middle. The leaves resemble those of true

Cinquefoil is more likely to invade a lawn when the soil is too acid. Shown here is Potentilla simplex.

strawberries, which have only three leaflets, white flowers, and delicious, juicy red fruit. The ground cover mock strawberry (*Duchesnea indica*) is also similar, but has three leaflets, yellow flowers, and small, spongy, tasteless, red berries.

Control Measures

In lawns: Rake up runners and mow close to the ground. Apply 2,4-D with or without dicamba (Ortho Weed-B-Gon® Lawn Weed Killer) or dichlorprop to kill cinquefoil. Prevent the weed by improving the soil with applications of fertilizer and lime as indicated by a soil analysis.

In gardens and around woody ornamentals: Hand-pull or cultivate to remove the weeds. Improve the soil by adding organic matter and a mulch. Apply lime as needed except under such acid-requiring plants as blueberry, rhododendron, and azalea.

CLOVER, WHITE

Trifolium repens
(White Dutch clover)

To keep or not to keep—that is the question when clover populates lawns. Clover has the unique ability to capture nitrogen from the air and add it to soil, so clover is sometimes considered desirable. In fact, for many years low-growing white clover was included in most lawn seed mixtures. However, clover flowers attract bees, and so-called grass stains can also be caused by clover leaves. In winter, patches of clover in lawns become bare except for their tough stems, thus providing an open place for winter annual weeds to grow.

Clover also volunteers readily in most turf sites, especially where cool-season grasses are cut too low. This delicate weed competes strongly with cool-season grasses already under stress in summer. It can spread rapidly through thin turf and invade other plantings.

The Weed

White clover has dark green three-leaflet leaves usually with a whitish mark near the base of each leaflet. The creeping stems of this shallow-rooted perennial legume root at nodes where they touch the soil. The little ball-shaped white or pink-tinted flowers peek above the leaves, detracting from the uniform appearance of a green lawn.

Control Measures

In lawns: Supplying enough nitrogen in spring and fall for vigorous turf growth helps the grass compete with clover. Limiting the amount of phosphorus applied may help. Control clover with a post-emergent spray of 2,4-D (Ortho Weed-B-Gon® Lawn Weed Killer, Ortho Chickweed, Spurge & Oxalis Killer D, Ortho Chickweed & Clover Control) in spring to prevent flowering. Keep the mower set high.

Welcome in lawns by some homeowners and not by others, white clover provides its own source of nitrogen and thus thrives in nitrogen-deficient soil.

In gardens: Cultivate as needed, and mulch to resist weed invasion and to make it easier to eliminate clover runners by hand-pulling. Where clover is a desired lawn component, install curbing or other barriers to keep the clover from moving out of the lawn and into other plantings.

Around woody ornamentals: Treat as indicated for gardens, or spot-spray glyphosate (Ortho Kleenup® Systemic Grass & Weed Killer).

COCKLEBUR

Xanthium species
(Clotbur, sheep bur, button bur)

Rough is a word that applies to all cockleburs, which feature rough heart-shaped leaves, rough woody stems with yellow sap, and rough seedpods, or burs. Burs have been spread from one part of the United States to another

in the coats of sheep and other animals. Cockleburs are troublesome along roadsides, in fields, and in other open or unmaintained areas.

The many similar-looking species are coarse warm-season annuals that can grow to 1 or 2 feet tall. Botanists classify them mainly by the shape, hairiness, and spininess of their burs. To gardeners they are all the same.

The Weed

Sterile and fertile flowers, both inconspicuous, occur in separate flower heads on the same plant. The two-celled, oval burs with strong, hooked spines contain two seeds in each compartment. The seeds germinate in consecutive years to increase survivability. The two-leafed seedlings are extremely poisonous, but this toxicity decreases as true leaves develop.

Beach clotbur (*Xanthium echinatum*), a weed of the seashore, is distinguished by purple-blotched stems and burs with two strong beaks curved inward at the tip.

Control Measures

In gardens and around woody ornamentals: Identify cocklebur seedlings by the bur remnant usually attached to the root at or below ground surface. Hoe the plants off at once to prevent seed set.

In unplanted seashore areas: Prevent the formation of beach clotbur seeds by spraying with 2,4-D and dicamba (Ortho Chickweed, Spurge & Oxalis Killer D).

The seeds of cocklebur are armed with mean, hooked spines that can anchor to fur or clothing.

CRABGRASS, SMOOTH AND LARGE

Digitaria ischaemum and
D. sanguinalis
(Finger grass, pigeon grass,
Polish millet)

The most troublesome of the lawn weeds, crabgrass is a shallow-rooted, warm-season annual grass. Introduced to the United States from Europe, it has made itself at home in every state. Smooth crabgrass (small crabgrass) is more common in northern areas, and large crabgrass (hairy crabgrass) predominates in southern and western regions. The husky, yellow-green seedlings may look attractive in early spring; but by midsummer, maturing plants branch and sprawl crablike, rooting firmly at nodes and sending up finger-shaped seed heads above coarse foliage that turns purple late in the season.

Crabgrass thrives under hot, dry conditions when cool-season grasses become semidormant; but it invades warm-season grasses too. With its coarse-textured leaves, crabgrass looks unsightly. Worse, it crowds out desirable grass, and when it dies in fall, open areas of brown stems allow enough light for seeds of winter annuals like common chickweed to germinate and grow. The following year when weather becomes hot and winter annuals die, dormant crabgrass seeds germinate in the bare spots they leave behind, repeating the cycle.

Crabgrass produces great quantities of seeds, ensuring its continued survival. This is especially troublesome when combating the weed because the seeds don't all germinate at the same time. Most germinate in spring but some remain dormant. Irrigation or rain after a dry spell can trigger germination right up until early fall.

Crabgrass is one of the worst lawn weeds in the United States; it can just as easily blanket a garden bed as a lawn. Shown is a plant of large crabgrass.

The Weed

These two species look much alike although they differ in size, degree of hairiness, and other botanical characteristics. Being able to tell them apart isn't important because control is the same for both.

To distinguish crabgrass seedlings from those of other common annual grasses, carefully bend a leaf blade away from the sheath that encircles the stem. There you will see the thin, telltale, membranous ligule (see page 11). Unlike crabgrass, the ligules of foxtail and fall panicum are mostly a fringe of hairs, and barnyardgrass has no ligule at all. Bermudagrass has long white hairs.

Control Measures

In lawns: The best time to control crabgrass is before it becomes a problem. In early spring a couple of weeks before the date predicted for crabgrass emergence in your area, apply a preemergent herbicide to prevent seeds from germinating. Researchers have found that crabgrass seeds, which have lain dormant all winter, begin to germinate when soil temperature reaches about 50° F. (This varies with different soil types and weather conditions.) Bare, compacted soil heats up fastest, and that is where the first slightly yellow-green crabgrass seedlings appear. More will appear in cooler sites, including thick turf, in a couple of weeks or so. For-

sythia flowers about the same time, so plan to make a pre-emergent application at least a couple of weeks before the forsythia blooms. In warm-weather areas two applications can be made: in late winter to prevent spring-germinating seeds, and in early fall just before the rainy season begins, to prevent fall-germinating weeds.

Benefin, bensulide, and DCPA (Dacthal®—Ortho Garden Weed Preventer) are recommended preemergent herbicides for use on lawns except those containing bentgrass, St. Augustine grass or centipedegrass. These pre-emergent herbicides will remain effective for three to four months or even longer, depending on soil and weather conditions.

Once crabgrass has germinated, control it with broadcast applications of a selective postemergent herbicide. Use a methanearsonate herbicide (Ortho Crabgrass Killer—Formula II, Ortho Crabgrass & Dandelion Killer). If applied as soon as crabgrass appears in the lawn and before seedlings are 2 inches tall, one

application should provide adequate control. For more mature crabgrass two applications 7 to 10 days apart will be needed. Applying a pre-emergent herbicide right after postemergent treatment in early summer can provide control for the remainder of the growing season, especially in areas where the season is a long one.

If there are only a few plants of crabgrass in the lawn, they can be treated with spot applications of methanearsonate (Ortho Crabgrass & Nutgrass Killer). Take care not to apply too much spray.

Crabgrass thrives in poorly grown, thin, or heat- and drought-stressed lawns. To encourage turf vigor, keep mower height set at 2 to 3 inches for cool-season grasses like Kentucky bluegrass or fine fescue and raise it to 3 inches in summer for tall fescue. This will shade the turf, preventing crabgrass seedlings from germinating. To help the turf resist invasion, thicken it by fertilizing adequately in fall and early spring and also in summer if recommended for

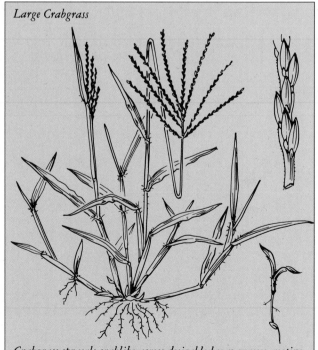

Large Crabgrass

Crabgrass sprawls crablike across desirable lawn grasses, rooting at the nodes. Late in the season, fingerlike seed heads (top right) rise above the coarse foliage. Seedlings (bottom right) germinate throughout the growing season.

your climate. Don't water lightly or too frequently—that encourages crabgrass germination and growth. Irrigate only when needed, watering deeply. Aerate heavy soils if needed.

In gardens: Prevent crabgrass germination in flower and vegetable beds by using DCPA (Dacthal®—Ortho Garden Weed Preventer) according to label directions. Cultivate beds regularly, leaving crabgrass roots exposed on the surface where they will dry out. If roots are left covered by soil they will continue to grow.

Around woody ornamentals: Maintain a thick mulch to shade out crabgrass, or cultivate shallowly and repeatedly. Spot-treat with the selective herbicide fluazifop-butyl (Ortho Grass-B-Gon® Grass Killer).

In walks, driveways, and patios: Glyphosate (Ortho Kleenup® Systemic Weed & Grass Killer, Ortho Kleenup® Spot Weed & Grass Killer) kills weeds growing in cracks. The nonselective herbicide prometon (Ortho Triox® Vegetation Killer) kills existing crabgrass and prevents seed germination for up to a year. Follow label directions carefully. The herbicide should not be applied over tree and shrub roots or near desirable plants.

CUDWEED

Gnaphalium species
(Cotton batting, everlasting, rabbit tobacco, lambsear)

Woolly plants in the daisy family, cudweeds are sometimes collected as everlastings. They primarily occur along roadways, in fields, in pastures, and in vacant lots, but they can invade gardens. The presence of cudweed in a garden indicates that the soil is in great need of improvement—it may be too dry, too wet, or infertile.

To dry cudweed for flower arrangements, cut before flower buds open. To control the weed look first to the condition of your soil, and improve it if need be.

The Weed
Cudweed species include annuals, winter annuals, and biennials, all of them characterized by white, woolly stems and narrow leaves that are green on top with woolly or silky hairs underneath. If not mowed, very small white flowers appear in crowded clusters on erect, branched stems. Some species are fragrant. Cudweed reproduces mainly by seeds, or in some species by rooting stems.

Control Measures
In lawns: Spray clumps with a product containing dicamba (Ortho Chickweed, Spurge & Oxalis Killer D). Control is best in spring when the weed is actively growing. In southern areas use a product containing MCPP (Ortho Weed-B-Gon® for Southern Lawns). Improve soil and begin good lawn management practices including proper fertilization.

In gardens and around woody ornamentals: Hand-pull large plants before they form seeds. Cultivate in spring, then mulch to maintain control. Improve soil by incorporating organic matter and fertilizing. Spot-treat with glyphosate (Ortho Kleenup® Grass & Weed Killer).

DALLISGRASS

Paspalum dilatatum
(Paspalumgrass, watergrass)

A perennial bunchgrass, dallisgrass has a coarse texture and tall unattractive seed-stalks that are objectionable in lawns. This weed occurs mostly in gardens and high-cut turf but can persist and spread when lawns are mowed too low. Thriving under warm moist conditions, dallisgrass grows in hot-summer areas of the United States from New Jersey to California.

The Weed
Dallisgrass has long coarse leaves whose stems radiate from the center of the plant. Plants form slightly spreading

Dallisgrass flowers are arranged on one side of the spikelets. The perennial grass is unattractive in lawns.

clumps with deep roots. Identify this grass by its firm membranous ligule (see page 11) at the base of the flat 1- to 4-inch-long leaf blades. The heavy seed heads are dense and oriented to one side, with roundish seeds on spreading spikelets. Dallisgrass reproduces primarily by seeds, but sometimes by its short rhizomes.

Control Measures
In lawns: There is no pre-emergent treatment registered for dallisgrass. In bermuda-grass or zoysiagrass lawns (but not bahiagrass) apply a post-emergent methanearsonate (Ortho Crabgrass Killer—Formula II for large areas; Ortho Crabgrass & Nutgrass Killer

for spot treatment) preferably in early spring or summer when dallisgrass is just starting vigorous growth; repeat two to four times at weekly intervals as needed. If hand-digging weeds, be sure to get well under the crown. Reseed bare spots.

In gardens and around woody ornamentals: Hand-pull or hoe shallowly. Mulch to keep new seedlings from becoming established. Spot-treat with glyphosate (Ortho Kleenup® Grass & Weed Killer). Prevent dallisgrass around flowers and woody ornamentals with dichlobenil (Ortho Casoron® Granules).

In walks, driveways, and patios: Spot-treat with glyphosate (Ortho Kleenup® Spot Weed & Grass Killer).

DANDELION

Taraxacum officinale
(Blowball, lionstooth, cankerwort, doon-head-clock)

The most common broadleaf weed in lawns and probably the most conspicuous, dandelion is a yellow-flowered perennial growing from a long fleshy taproot. It occurs worldwide. One reason it is difficult to control is that new shoots quickly develop from even a small piece of remaining root when the weed is hand-pulled or cut at the crown.

The Weed

The deep fleshy taproot produces a stemless rosette of irregularly lobed or toothed leaves of varying lengths. The leaves remain close to the ground throughout the year. Yellow flower heads are borne singly on unbranched hollow stems whose length depends on temperature. They remain flush with the ground during cool spring and fall weather and lengthen as weather becomes warmer. The flowers bloom when days are short and nights long in spring and again in autumn, but they seldom appear in summer when the reverse is true. Roots, leaves, and flower stems have milky juice.

Fluffy tufts of fine hairs carry the seeds in the wind like little parachutes, sometimes for miles, before being deposited to start new plants.

Control Measures

In lawns: Eliminate established dandelions by applying 2,4-D (Ortho Weed-B-Gon® Lawn Weed Killer, Ortho Chickweed, Spurge & Oxalis Killer D, Ortho Crabgrass & Dandelion Killer) anytime

Close-cut lawns are more likely to be invaded by this most common of lawn weeds, the dandelion. Set mower blades higher to discourage it.

dandelions are actively growing. Control is least effective when dandelions are in full bloom. It is best to apply the herbicide early in spring before blossoms form, and repeat in very early fall to eliminate any misses and new seedlings. If dandelions reappear a single application in fall will eliminate them as a problem. Spot-treat with 2,4-D (Ortho Weed-B-Gon® Jet Weeder—Formula II, Ortho Weed-B-Gon® Weed Killer) if there are only a few dandelions. Thickening turf by fertilizing properly and mow-

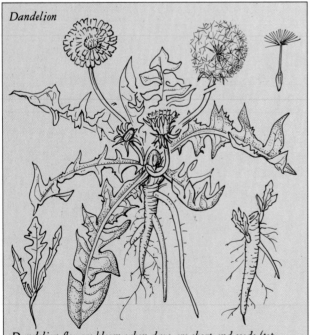

Dandelion

Dandelion flowers bloom when days are short and seeds (top right) float through the air and are carried long distances. Seedlings (bottom left) germinate throughout the growing season. If broken, the deep taproot (bottom right) can sprout new plants from even a tiny piece.

ing high enough will discourage new seedlings.

In gardens and around woody ornamentals: Mulch or cultivate regularly to prevent seedling establishment. Carefully pull existing dandelions or cut out the entire root by digging deeply with an asparagus knife.

DEADNETTLE

Lamium purpureum
(Purple deadnettle, red deadnettle)

A winter annual or biennial similar to its more common close relative, henbit (see page 64), deadnettle grows in lawns and landscaped areas where soil is rich. This pest, related to a garden ground cover, is distributed commonly in eastern North America but is infrequent in western states.

The Weed

The almost triangular leaves have scalloped edges and short hairs on the surface. All the petioles (leafstalks) bend downward. Upper leaves are usually purplish and crowded, and have short petioles. The lower part of the squarish stem tends to lie on the ground and may root at

Purple deadnettle has the squarish stem and two-lipped flowers typical of the mint family. Upper leaves are usually purplish.

nodes. Small, purple, lipped flowers bloom in a few clusters at the tip, mostly in very early spring but sometimes in late winter. The weed grows 4 to 12 inches tall.

Control Measures

In lawns: Treat early with a spray containing dicamba (Ortho Chickweed, Spurge & Oxalis Killer D). Keep flowering heads cut to prevent formation of seeds.

In gardens and around woody ornamentals: Deadnettle seeds germinate only in fall. Cultivate shallowly then to minimize the weed's appearance and growth over the winter.

DICHONDRA

Dichondra repens

A perennial from the tropics, dichondra grows only in warm climates. In southern California it makes an attractive lawn substitute if irrigated

A lawn grass substitute in mild climates, dichondra is an annoying weed when it invades grass lawns.

regularly and fertilized. Only 1 to 2 inches tall, dichondra rarely requires mowing. In most other regions, a dichondra lawn becomes thin and weedy, and can invade grass lawns, gardens, and shrub borders.

The Weed

Dichondra has smooth, erect, kidney-shaped leaves and slender, runnerlike stems that root freely, forming mats. Petioles (leafstalks) grow longer in shaded areas, but dichondra will spread rapidly in sun or shade. From March through May small, inconspicuous flowers form below the leaves in axils (the angle formed by juncture of leaf and stem).

Control Measures

In lawns: Where it has become a weed, eliminate dichondra with a postemergent application of 2,4-D or a product containing 2,4-D and dicamba (Ortho Weed-B-Gon® Lawn Weed Killer). Use MCPP (Ortho Weed-B-Gon® for Southern Lawns) on warm-season grasses.

In gardens and around woody ornamentals: Pull by hand or rake the shallow-rooted runners out. Prevent the weed with dichlobenil (Ortho Casoron® Granules) around listed ornamentals.

DODDER

Cuscuta species
(Strangleweed, lovevine, devils hair)

There are over a dozen highly specialized species of this parasitic plant in North America. (Over 100 species exist world-wide). Having no chlorophyll and thus unable to survive alone, dodders use other plants as hosts. Like parasitic spaghetti, the stringy mass of yellow-to-orange viny stems can envelop a host by late summer. As dodder grows, it branches and rebranches rapidly, spreading from plant to plant. Any growing section of dodder is independent of any other, gaining its nourishment locally and continuing to grow.

Dodder is common on legumes, especially alfalfa. The wide range of host plants also includes tomato, onion, carrot, blueberry, cranberry, petunia, periwinkle, azalea, and other shrubs and herbs. A heavy infestation of dodder can prevent a plant from forming fruit.

The Weed

The threadlike, leafless dodder seedling arches from the soil, straightens out, and begins to imperceptibly rotate counterclockwise around any

Ghostly yellow strands of the parasitic weed dodder have almost covered these mugwort plants.

object within 1 to 3 inches that it touches. If the object touched is not a suitable host, the seedling dies. If the object is the stem of a suitable host plant, suckerlike roots penetrate the stem and begin robbing the plant of the nutrients and water it carries. The lower part of the dodder then shrivels and the connection to the soil is lost.

Abundant clusters of small white flowers and hard seeds are produced as new branches continuously form throughout the growing season. Seed germination is irregular.

Control Measures

Wherever found: There is no selective way to remove dodder from the infested part of its host. Both must be destroyed to prevent further infestation. Even tiny pieces of dodder that remain on a plant continue to grow, so don't try to pull it off. Cut below the point at which the dodder is attached, remove the cut vegetation, and burn it. Never compost dodder.

A preemergent application of dichlobenil (Casoron®) or a high application rate of DCPA (Dacthal®) to the soil containing dodder seeds prevents seedling emergence. Dodder can also be prevented by keeping the area cleanly cultivated or mulched.

ENGLISH DAISY

Bellis perennis
(European daisy, March daisy, boneflower)

Spread by seeds and pieces of rootstock, this winsome perennial plant is often grown as an ornamental, but it sometimes escapes from cultivation and becomes a difficult-to-control weed. The weed problem develops chiefly in lawns and gardens in cool, moist regions of the West Coast. English daisy is resented on golf courses where its leaves disturb the surface of putting greens and its flowers can be mistaken for golf balls from a distance.

The Weed

Leaves of the small, low plants are slightly toothed, have broad tips, and are narrower toward the base. They

Some enjoy seeing the cheery English daisy in a lawn; others, particularly golfers, prefer solid green.

form basal rosettes from which flower heads emerge on leafless stems. Blossoms may be single or double with white, pink, or red petals

surrounding yellow centers. They bloom in sunny places, mainly in mid- to late spring.

Control Measures

In lawns: Use 2,4-D (Ortho Weed-B-Gon® Lawn Weed Killer) or 2,4-D and dicamba (Ortho Chickweed, Spurge & Oxalis Killer D) for postemergent control. Treat in spring and again in early fall to control any regrowth and new seedlings. Fertilize to thicken turf.

In gardens and around woody ornamentals: Cultivate to cut the fibrous roots under the rosettes. The plants can also be dug up, transplanted, and enjoyed in the garden border or a window box.

FALL PANICUM

Panicum dichotomiflorum
(Spreading panicgrass, smooth witchgrass, sprouting crabgrass)

An annual grass with coarse, fibrous roots, fall panicum can be troublesome in garden beds, in newly established lawns, and in areas kept mowed low.

The Weed

One or many smooth stems may zigzag at the nodes and grow upright, spread, or lie nearly flat on the ground with only the tips upright. Lower nodes are swollen and may root on the ground. Leaves of young plants are slightly hairy but later ones are smooth. The ligule (see page 11) is a fringe of short hairs, and leaf blades have an identifying, prominent midvein. *P. capillare* (old witchgrass, tumblegrass, hairgrass) is a similar annual but quite hairy, as the common name indicates.

The delicate, bushy, pyramidal flower clusters and seed heads of both weeds appear from summer to early fall. When mature these break off and tumble about, dropping their seeds.

Fall panicum is a grassy annual weed with a loose airy seed head that breaks off and rolls around, scattering its seeds.

Control Measures
In gardens and around woody ornamentals: To prevent the weed apply DCPA (Dacthal®— Ortho Garden Weed Preventer) to clean ground before seeds start germinating in late spring. Apply fluazifop-butyl (Ortho Grass-B-Gon® Grass Killer) to established fall panicum.

Hand-pull or hoe young weeds while they are small; the shallow roots are easy to pull up. The soil can be cultivated repeatedly as seeds continue to germinate through the season, or seed emergence can easily be suppressed by mulching. Mow nearby fields before a new crop of seeds form and spread into cultivated areas.

FESCUE, TALL

Festuca arundinacea
(Kentucky 31 fescue)

Formerly added to lawn seed mixtures as a nurse grass, this coarse perennial clump grass has come to be regarded as a weed because of its unattractive contrast with fine turfgrasses. Because it is tough and relatively heat-resistant, it is still used as a turfgrass in transitional zones where summers tend to be too hot and dry for good Kentucky bluegrass growth and where winters are too cold and long for warm-season grasses to thrive.

Although tall fescue doesn't have runners (the short rootstalks creep only a bit) single plants growing in lawns lie flat and thus look wide and unattractive.

The Weed
The long leaf blades form a 90-degree angle with the stems, and their dull upper surfaces are ridged. Tall fescue is easily distinguished from other coarse grasses by the tiny stiff hairs along the leaf margins that catch at your fingers when you stroke upward along them.

Control Measures
In lawns: Remove young clumps by cutting under the root crown, or carefully spot-spray these and larger, older clumps with glyphosate (Ortho Kleenup® Systemic Weed & Grass Killer). Reseed or replace with sod if the clump was large.

In gardens: Hand-pull as soon as the weed is noticed, undercutting the root crown to sever the heavy fibrous roots, or cautiously spot-treat with glyphosate (Ortho Kleenup® Systemic Weed & Grass Killer) according to label restrictions.

Tall fescue lies flat in a lawn, eluding mower blades and looking unattractive.

Around woody ornamentals: Apply fluazifop-butyl (Ortho Grass-B-Gon® Grass Killer) for selective control of fescue and other grasses growing with listed shrubs, ground covers, and other ornamentals.

FLORIDA BEGGARWEED

Desmodium tortuosum
(Stick-tight, beggar lice, beggartick)

This annual weed was probably introduced from the West Indies and is now found throughout Florida, along coastal areas, inland from Texas to North Carolina, and in Hawaii. Its sticky seed heads adhere tenaciously to socks and pant legs.

The Weed
The growth of this weed, which has a taproot, is upright and multi-branched. Stems are rounded and usually covered densely with short, stiff hairs that may be reddish purple. Its small, purple, pea-like flowers

Florida beggarweed is one of the many weeds whose seeds hitch a ride on fur or clothing. Even lightly brushing by it can dislodge the annoying seeds.

show this weed's relationship to other legumes. Seeds in the flat, deeply jointed pod have hooked hairs so they stick to clothing like those of its perennial relative, tick trefoil (*D. canescens*). Creeping beggarweed (*D. canum*) is another similar perennial; its stems and leaves grow close to the ground with clusters of small, purplish, pea-like flow-

ers and seeds forming on upright stalks.

Control Measures
In lawns: Spray a postemergent herbicide containing MCPP (Ortho Weed-B-Gon® for Southern Lawns). St. Augustine grass may be temporarily discolored or injured. Fertilize adequately to thicken turf. Mow creeping beggarweed to keep it low.

In gardens and around woody ornamentals: Cultivate early to eliminate seedlings. Mulch to continue control. Spot-treat with glyphosate (Ortho Kleenup® Grass & Weed Killer) according to label directions.

FLORIDA BETONY

Stachys floridana
(Rattlesnake weed, Florida artichoke)

A nuisance in lawns, garden beds and other landscaped areas, Florida betony spreads rapidly during the winter and spring in the South. Hot summer weather causes the tops to die. Seeds germinate and tubers begin new growth in the fall.

The Weed
This perennial has the four-sided stems typical of the mint family to which it belongs. Its oval leaves are slightly hairy and have toothed edges. Two-lipped white, pink, or purple flowers bloom from spring into early summer, maturing into smooth seeds in about a month. Florida betony branches freely aboveground, especially in lawns where it is kept low by mowing. Underground its slender rhizomes end in grub-shaped white tubers whose dark, constricting rings suggest snake rattles.

Control Measures
In lawns: Use 2,4-D and dicamba (Ortho Chickweed Spurge & Oxalis Killer D) or

The rattler-shaped tubers of Florida betony earned it the common name rattlesnake weed.

MCPP (Ortho Weed-B-Gon® for Southern Lawns) in spring when Florida betony is growing actively.

In gardens: Cultivate to remove tubers as they are turned up and to prevent seedling establishment. Discourage the weed by covering with landscape fabric or black plastic mulch.

Around woody ornamentals: Apply glyphosate (Ortho Kleenup® Systemic Weed & Grass Killer) to eliminate patches. Apply a preemergent herbicide containing dichlobenil (Ortho Casoron® Granules) or EPTC (Eptam®) to the soil in September to prevent seed germination. Where shallow cultivation is possible, remove tubers brought to the surface. Prevent emergence with dichlobenil (Ortho Casoron® Granules).

FLORIDA PUSLEY

Richardia scabra
(Florida purslane, Mexican clover, pussley)

A summer annual with a taproot and fibrous roots near the surface, Florida pusley is a weed in the southeastern coastal states from North Carolina to Florida and west to Texas. Preferring dry, sandy soils, its low, dense clumps crowd out desirable plants in lawns and beds and invade cracks in pavement.

The Weed
Fine, soft hairs cover this weed's reddish brown stems. Its leaves are flat, untoothed, oval to lance-shaped, and opposite each other. When growing upright it develops few branches; when growing low it develops many spreading branches. Stubby clusters of small, six-pointed tubular white flowers appear at the base of the upper leaf axils (angle between leaf and stem) from late spring until early autumn.

Florida pusley can be confused with Virginia buttonweed (see page 89), a weed becoming more prevalent in the southeastern states. (Flowers of the latter have only four petals and they occur singly in leaf axils.)

Control Measures
In lawns: The weed is readily controlled by postemergent application of 2,4-D and MCPP (Ortho Weed-B-Gon® Lawn Weed Killer for large areas; Ortho Weed B-Gon®

Florida pusley, a weed of southeastern coastal states, produces clusters of six-petaled white flowers.

Jet Weeder—Formula II for spot treatment), 2,4-D with dicamba (Ortho Chickweed, Spurge & Oxalis Killer D), or MCPP (Ortho Weed-B-Gon® for Southern Lawns). It can also be spot-treated with 2,4-D (Ortho Weed-B-Gon® Weed Killer). Improve soil where possible and follow good management practices to thicken turf and make it more resistant to invasion.

In gardens: To keep the weeds from developing and producing more seeds, hand-pull or cultivate repeatedly wherever Florida pusley seedlings appear.

Around woody ornamentals: Apply DCPA (Dacthal®—Ortho Garden Weed Preventer) as a preemergent control in early spring. Cultivate or apply dichlobenil (Ortho Casoron® Granules) to cleared soil in late fall or very early spring before the weather turns warm. Keep well mulched to resist further invasion.

FOXTAIL, GREEN AND YELLOW

Setaria viridis and *S. glauca*, syn. *S. lutescens*
(Bristlegrass, pigeongrass)

Forming tufts in lawns and gardens, this coarse-leaved weedy annual grass troubles gardeners throughout the United States. It spreads by seeds and is most annoying in yards bordering unmaintained lots, fields, and roadways.

The Weed
Foxtail is a weedy fibrous-rooted grass often mistaken for crabgrass (see page 56) when immature. Tell foxtail apart from crabgrass and other common weedy grasses by examining the ligule (see page 11). Gently hold the leaf blade away from the stem to look at the attachment. Foxtail has a little fringe of hairs, crabgrass has a thin membrane, and barnyardgrass (see page 11) has no ligule at all. Seedling foxtail leaves are more slender than the other weedy grasses.

Differences between foxtail and crabgrass become more obvious later in the summer. Foxtail is mostly upright or somewhat spreading at the lower nodes but doesn't creep and root as crabgrass does. Identities become clear if the weeds are allowed to reach maturity. Foxtail seed heads are dense bushy spikes with short bristles, giving the weed its common name. Green foxtail's three or fewer bristles per spikelet are green to slightly purple and its leaves are smooth. Yellow foxtail has five bristles per spikelet that glisten golden in the sun, long kinky hairs at the base of the leaves, and leaf sheaths that may be reddish toward the base.

Control Measures
In lawns: Foxtail seeds are dormant in the fall, germinating in the spring and early summer. Prevent emergence with a spring application of benefin, DCPA (Dacthal®—Ortho Garden Weed Preventer), or trifluralin. Treat emerged plants with methanearsonates (Ortho Crabgrass Killer—Formula II

Foxtail is an annual grass, growing only from seeds dropped by the bristly seed heads. Here sunlight is shining through yellow foxtail.

for large areas; Ortho Crabgrass & Nutgrass Killer for spot treatment). Do not use on St. Augustine grass, centipedegrass, and carpetgrass. Foxtail is not as aggressive as crabgrass and can be eliminated by improving turf quality.

In gardens: Buried seeds germinate most readily the

next year. After cultivating the top inch of soil, apply benefin, DCPA (Dacthal®—Ortho Garden Weed Preventer) or trifluralin around listed plants. Regular cultivation that leaves foxtail roots exposed works; those merely disturbed will reroot.

Around woody ornamentals: Spot-treat in ground covers and under shrubs with the selective herbicide fluazifop-butyl (Ortho Grass-B-Gon® Grass Killer) or glyphosate (Ortho Kleenup® Grass & Weed Killer) as directed on the label. Regular shallow cultivation helps. A permanent mulch should eliminate the need for other controls.

GALINSOGA, HAIRY AND SMALLFLOWER

Galinsoga ciliata and *G. parviflora* (Quickweed)

These two annual weeds reproduce very quickly from seeds, especially in rich, moist cultivated soil—hence their other common name, quickweed. One or the other species may predominate or they may be mixed together. Neither of these shallow-rooted weeds is a strong competitor with vegetables or ornamental flowering plants, although they have other habits that make them noxious.

They flower and mature throughout the growing season appearing from midspring until frost. A seedling grows so quickly that it can form its own crop of seeds six to seven weeks after germination. Having no period of dormancy, seeds germinate only a week or two after they reach the surface of moist soil. This cycle from germination to seed formation can be repeated three to five times a year depending on the length of the growing season. Thus populations are constantly

Hairy galinsoga is a weed not to be ignored, since it can set seed and regrow continuously all season long.

renewed and the weed can create an unsightly garden if not controlled. Galinsoga is also an alternate host for certain nematodes and viruses (see page 7).

The Weed

Stems grow upright to about a foot tall and form branches opposite each other. Leaves are opposite, rotated 90 degrees at each node, oval, and pointed at the tips. Galinsoga bears numerous ⅛- to ¼-inch-long somewhat daisylike flowers at the ends of the branches. Hairy galinsoga lives up to its name with hairier stems and leaves that are toothed. It tends to be denser and shorter than smallflower galinsoga, which lives up to its name by having slightly smaller flowers. Less hairy, it has more open growth and leaves with wavy margins.

Control Measures

In lawns: Galinsoga can invade new lawns. Control with a postemergent application of 2,4-D (Ortho Chickweed, Spurge & Oxalis Killer D).

In gardens: Neither galinsoga species responds to treatment with available preemergent herbicides. Herbicides don't do a good job of controlling the weed because new seedlings constantly germinate. With galinsoga, whose seeds are mostly in the top ½ inch of soil, the best control is frequent light

cultivation before seedlings are more than 2 to 3 inches tall; severed pieces of galinsoga root are able to form new plants so these should be raked off and put in the compost pile. Mulching can also prevent emergence of new seedlings.

GOOSEGRASS

Eleusine indica
(Silver crabgrass, yardgrass, wiregrass, crowfootgrass, bullgrass)

A tough summer annual, goosegrass is a stubborn problem most often where soil has been compacted by heavy foot traffic or in very open turf. Goosegrass can form seeds from early summer until late fall. It germinates in midspring two or more weeks later than crabgrass when soil temperatures warm up to 60° to 65° F.

In warm, sunny sites goosegrass is most competitive with any turf thinned by close mowing, excessive wear, frequent watering, or lack of

Flattened stems that are silvery at the base characterize goosegrass, an annual lawn weed able to grow even on a hard-packed path or on a tennis court.

fertilizer. In thin warm-season turf, especially at its northern limits, goosegrass may replace annual bluegrass, invading open spaces left as that weed dies. Warmth and high light at that time favor goosegrass germination.

The Weed

Seedlings have smooth, distinctly flattened stems that are pale whitish green or silver at the base with darker green blades. The ligule (see page

11) is shorter than that of crabgrass and rather ragged. It does not root at nodes but grows only as tufts with branching stems radiating from the center. Stems of young plants lie almost flat on the ground. They are more erect as the grass matures and forms fingerlike seed heads that are heavier than those of crabgrass. These radiate from the top of the stem and often a single finger emerges lower on the stem.

Control Measures

In lawns: Aerate heavy soil. Reroute or pave areas compacted by heavy foot traffic or recreational use. Crabgrass herbicides do not satisfactorily control goosegrass. To prevent serious goosegrass problems, it is necessary to build turf density by good lawn management and to rely on methanarsonates (Ortho Crabgrass Killer—Formula II) only for moderate control. Where only a few weeds occur, remove them by hand or spot-treat with glyphosate (Ortho Kleenup® Spot Weed & Grass Killer) to prevent the weeds from reseeding.

In gardens: Use the preemergent DCPA (Dacthal®—Ortho Garden Weed Preventer) according to label directions. Where soil is loose goosegrass seldom becomes the problem it can be in turf. Cultivate shallowly, cutting below the root crown as soon as goosegrass seedlings begin to appear; mulch to prevent further germination.

Around woody ornamentals: Spot-treat with fluazifop-butyl (Ortho Grass-B-Gon® Grass Killer) or glyphosate (Ortho Kleenup® Grass & Weed Killer) around listed plants. Then apply a heavy mulch.

In walks, driveways, patios, etc.: Treat with a combination of glyphosate and oxyfluorfen (Ortho Kleenup® Super Edger). In areas that will be kept free of all vegetation and away from tree or shrub roots, apply the nonselective herbicide prometon (Ortho Triox® Vegetation Killer).

GROUND-CHERRY, SMOOTH

Physalis subglabrata
(Husk tomato)

If not controlled this weed can grow to 1 to 2 feet tall in vegetable and ornamental beds. It attracts cucumber and flea beetles to the garden; these eat holes in ground-cherry leaves as well as related vegetables like tomato and eggplant. About a dozen groundcherry species can be troublesome; perennial species reproduce by seed and by stout, deeply penetrating, widely spreading roots.

The Weed
Stems are erect and branched in the upper part, giving them the appearance of a miniature tree. The drooping bell-shaped flowers are yellow, often with dark markings at the center. They appear from midsummer until early fall. By late summer small round edible berries develop within ribbed papery balloons similar to the orange ones on ornamental Chinese lantern plants. Each berry has many flattened seeds resembling those of tomato.

Control Measures
In gardens: None of the major postemergent herbicides—2,4-D, dicamba, and

This smooth groundcherry plant shows damage by flea beetles, a pest that can harm garden plants as well.

glyphosate—controls groundcherry satisfactorily. DCPA (Dacthal®) can be applied to clean ground to prevent seedling emergence but has no effect on emerged groundcherry. If seedlings appear later, clean-cultivate and once more apply DCPA. Hand-pull the weeds, cultivate to remove as much of the fleshy creeping rootstock as possible, or keep cutting off the tops to starve the roots. Continue to pull out, grub, or hoe the weeds until late in the garden year, even after the last cultivation.

GROUND IVY

Glechoma hederacea
(Gill-over-the-ground, creeping-charlie, field balm)

Common in eastern, southeastern, and midwestern states, this perennial creeper is attractive enough to be sometimes used as a ground cover, although its aggressiveness identifies it as a weed. The long trailing stems produce shallow roots and branches at each node, enabling the plant to quickly invade large areas. Ground ivy forms dense patches in lawns and garden areas. It grows well in sun even though it prefers shade and somewhat damp places where turfgrasses may not do well.

The Weed
The squarish stems and distinct odor quickly identify ground ivy as a member of the mint family. Leaves are opposite, rounded, slightly hairy, and heavily veined with scalloped edges. From late spring to early summer, clusters of cheerful, tubular, two-lipped purplish flowers bloom in leaf axils (angle formed by leaf and stem); these produce seeds that can germinate immediately. The weed also reproduces by pieces of broken runners.

Control Measures
In lawns: Catch infestations early to minimize the amount of control needed. Ground ivy responds only fairly well

A mint family member, ground ivy spreads by long horizontal stems, rooting and branching at every leaf node.

to applications of 2,4-D or MCPP separately. More effective are combinations of 2,4-D, MCPP, 2,4-DP, or triclopyr (Ortho Weed-B-Gon® Lawn Weed Killer, Ortho Chickweed & Clover Control for large areas; Ortho-Weed-B-Gon® Jet Weeder—Formula II, or Weed-B-Gon® Weed Killer for spot treatment). Early spring and fall are recommended as application times. Repeat the treatment if control is not complete, because remnants of rooted stems will continue the infestation. Where dense mats have formed, complete control may take two years.

In gardens: Since rooting is shallow, cultivating with a potato hook or similar tool

to raise and remove runners helps eliminate ground ivy; remove all pieces of stem or the weed will resprout.

Around woody ornamentals: Cultivate or apply the herbicide as in gardens or install a smothering landscape fabric mulch. Spot-treat with glyphosate (Ortho Kleenup® Grass & Weed Killer) according to label restrictions. Prevent ground ivy with dichlobenil (Ortho Casoron® Granules) applied in winter.

GROUNDSEL, COMMON

Senecio vulgaris
(Grimsel, ragwort, old-man-in-the-spring)

This common weed flowers and produces seeds from late spring until late fall. The seeds germinate in cool, wet weather. Groundsel prefers rich, moist soil and can pop up in garden beds in almost any part of the United States.

The Weed
Common groundsel, which has a fairly strong taproot, may grow as a single stalk or it may branch from the base. The stems and leaves are smooth and somewhat fleshy. The raggedly lobed leaves are alternate; lower ones are stalked but upper ones clasp the stem. If the weed reaches maturity, its clusters of small tightly cylindrical flower heads help identify it; the flowers lack the showy petals of most other groundsels and daisies. When the seeds are mature, common groundsel looks as if it is holding up little powder puffs because each seed has five straight silky hairs attached to it. These can soar long distances on an air current.

Control Measures
In gardens and around woody ornamentals: Groundsel plants can be killed with

Groundsel seeds ripen even after the weed is pulled from the ground, a good reason to get rid of young plants before they bloom.

Healall flowers open from behind overlapping bracts, forming dense heads at the tops of square stems.

glyphosate (Ortho Kleenup® Systemic Weed & Grass Killer) in ornamental beds. In vegetable gardens, it may be better to eliminate this weed by cultivating during the growing season to kill it and prevent formation of more seeds. In cold-winter areas keep the soil continually stirred through late fall to stimulate germination of as many seedlings as possible. These are soon destroyed by frost.

HAWKWEED, YELLOW AND ORANGE

Hieracium pratense and *H. aurantiacum*
(King devil and devil's paintbrush)

Of the several hawkweeds that immigrated to the United States from Europe, yellow hawkweed is the most abundant followed by orange hawkweed. They are pretty occupants of fields and dry roadsides but can be troublesome invaders of poorly grown lawns. The presence of hawkweeds is a give-away that the soil is dry, infertile, acid, and compacted. Hawkweeds are perennials that reproduce by seeds and short leafy runners. Seeds usually only germinate in compacted soil.

The Weed
Both species have rosettes of oblong leaves with upper and lower surfaces covered with short bristly hairs. Their flowers appear all summer in clusters of a dozen at the ends of leafless or one-leafed stalks. These resemble small yellow or orange dandelions and their seeds also have little plumes for wind dispersal.

Control Measures
In lawns: Eliminate patches of hawkweed with a combination of 2,4-D and dicamba (Ortho Chickweed, Spurge & Oxalis Killer D) or 2,4-D and 2,4-DP since 2,4-D alone is not enough. Plan far enough ahead so that thin or bare spots can be reseeded; apply lime and fertilizer as indicated by a soil analysis. Aerate the

Yellow hawkweed could be mistaken for dandelion, but its leaves are unlobed and hairy, unlike those of dandelion.

soil in compacted areas. If the problem is serious, you may want to renovate completely by killing the lawn with glyphosate and improving the soil with considerable amounts of organic matter.

In gardens: Eradicate any hawkweed as soon as detected. Improve the soil with water-holding organic matter; fertilize and add lime as in-

dicated by soil analysis. Keep the soil loosened with regular cultivation.

Around woody ornamentals: Cut off the tops before seeds form; discard tops to avoid their rooting again. Keep the area shallow cultivated until fall. Fertilize as needed and add lime except under acid-loving shrubs such as azalea, rhododendron, and blueberry.

HEALALL

Prunella vulgaris
(Self-heal, carpenterweed)

Spreading rapidly in moist lawns, healall troubles lawns and gardens throughout North America. This mint-family member is slender and leggy with pale flowers when it grows in shade. In sun growth is shorter and more compact and flowers are a darker color. When mowed repeatedly or constantly trampled, healall becomes densely matted and growth is lower with smaller leaves. There are many variations in hairiness, flower color, and leaf shape but in all cases the weed spreads by seeds and short runners that root where nodes touch soil. The weed blooms from spring until frost as new shoots develop; it remains green through the winter.

The Weed
A low perennial, healall's most distinctive features are its sharply ridged square stems and its thick spikes of lipped violet to purplish flowers. The flowers peer from beneath overlapping green or purplish bracts fringed with bristly white hairs. Leaves, two at a node, are mostly elliptical with smooth margins and sometimes a purple cast.

Control Measures
In lawns: Neither 2,4-D nor dicamba provides wholly satisfactory control when used alone. When combined

(Ortho Chickweed, Spurge & Oxalis Killer D) their control is excellent. Early fall is the most effective time to treat the prostrate patches.

In gardens and around woody ornamentals: Healall seldom persists under cultivation and can be eliminated by shallow hoeing that undercuts all the roots of the creeping runners.

HENBIT

Lamium amplexicaule
(Dead nettle, blind nettle, bee nettle, giraffe head)

Usually a fibrous-rooted winter annual, henbit occasionally acts as a biennial or even a short-lived perennial. It reproduces primarily by seeds. Seedlings begin germinating in early fall from seeds dropped earlier; these survive cold weather and may start flowering during warm spells in late winter, becoming more and more conspicuous in gardens and brown lawns of dormant warm-season lawns. This weed occurs throughout most of the United States, especially in rich garden soil.

The Weed
Square stems lie close to the ground at the base, then curve and grow upright, and often root at lower nodes. The bottom pairs of leaves have long stalks and don't bend downward as do those of purple deadnettle (see page 58). Upper leaves are stalkless,

clasping the stem to form a little green ruff for the nosegays of two-lipped tubular flowers that poke out above the upper leaf axils (angle formed by leaf and stem). The flower's top lip is arched, has a tuft of hair at the apex, and may glow ruby red although the rest of the flower is pinkish or purplish.

Control Measures

In lawns: Try to eliminate seedlings in fall by treating them with MCPP alone or a combination of 2,4-D, MCPP, 2,4-DP, or dicamba (Ortho Weed-B-Gon® Lawn Weed Killer, Ortho Chickweed, Spurge & Oxalis Killer D) on listed lawn grasses. On sensitive warm-season turf use MCPP alone (Ortho Weed-B-Gon® for Southern Lawns). Easily eliminate scattered henbit plants on *fully dormant* bermudagrass or other warm-season lawns by spot-treating with a combination of MCPP and 2,4-D (Ortho Weed-B-Gon® Jet Weeder—Formula II). Bensulide can be applied in late summer or early fall as

The ruffled leaves of henbit clasp the stem in oppositely arranged pairs.

a preemergent treatment to prevent henbit. Use good management practices to keep the lawn thick and weed-free.

In gardens and around woody ornamentals: Cultivate early in spring to remove existing plants and prevent seed formation. Follow with

shallow surface cultivation in early fall to destroy new seedlings. Year-round mulch will smother seedlings. Fall application of dichlobenil (Ortho Casoron® Granules) can be used on clean ground under many woody ornamentals if the henbit problem is severe. Kill existing weeds and prevent new ones from germinating with a combination of glyphosate and oxyfluorfen (Ortho Kleenup® Super Edger).

HORSENETTLE

Solanum carolinense
(Carolina nettle, bull nettle, wild tomato, apple-of-Sodom)

This weed employs a diverse barrage of survival and reproductive techniques. Its roots go 8 feet deep and extend out 3 to 4 feet in the upper 18 inches of soil. A new plant can grow from a ¼-inch-thick piece of root less than an inch long or from a bud 12 inches down on the taproot, assuring continuation in spite of mechanical attempts at eradication. Dense stands of horsenettle that evolve where the weed is undisturbed resist most attempts at controlling the pest.

Horsenettle is a particular problem in lawns and beds where former farmland is becoming residential. The weed is a host for insects and diseases of several important vegetables including two of its close relatives, tomato and potato.

The Weed

A member of the nightshade family, horsenettle grows upright and usually branches. Leaves are unevenly lobed or toothed. Sharply pointed yellowish spines on the main stem, on branches, and on the leaf midrib and lateral veins add to the unpleasantness of this weed.

Horsenettle, a perennial relative of tomato and potato, harbors many insects and diseases that also attack these domestic plants.

Its large, white to purplish star-shaped flowers have five conspicuous yellow anthers. These produce smelly yellow berries that are poisonous to cattle. (There have been no substantiated reports of human poisoning.) The berries produce large numbers of seeds, which don't need light for germination; these sprout from midspring to the end of summer from as deep as 4 inches in the soil.

Control Measures

In lawns: Continually keeping tops removed by regular mowing eventually exhausts the roots. Horsenettle is difficult to kill with herbicides; the best response is from spot-treating with glyphosate in the early bloom stage when root reserves are low. Repeat if needed.

In gardens and around woody ornamentals: Constant cultivation is necessary up until hard frost; keep tops cut so there are no leaves to manufacture food and consequently no new seeds formed. Mulching is little help with this aggressive pest. Glyphosate plus oxyfluorfen (Ortho Kleenup® Super Edger) can be used around woody ornamentals to control existing weeds and prevent further germination for up to three months.

HORSETAIL, FIELD

Equisetum arvense
(Horsetail fern, meadowpine, pinegrass, scouringrush, bottlebrush, snakegrass, devilsguts)

This fern ally is a primitive plant harking back to the days of dinosaurs. It forms no flowers and no seeds; instead, it reproduces by spores. Horsetail spreads mainly from extensive dark brown or black underground stems with tubers often 3 feet below the ground surface.

Field horsetail is found most often in wet sandy or gravelly soils as well as along streamsides and on railroad embankments. The plant can spread agressively and invade lawns and gardens.

The Weed

Tubers produce two types of shoots. Both are jointed, hollow, and can be pulled apart

Top: In very early spring field horsetail sends up whitish stems, topped with odd-looking brown spore-bearing cones.
Bottom: Field horsetail is such a primitive plant that it has no leaves, just lacy green whorls of jointed stems.

and fitted back together. In very early spring slender whitish unbranched stems appear, ending in a brownish cone where the spores are formed. Branches on this type are reduced to a very short sheath with black-tipped teeth. After the spores are shed in midspring, these stems die down and the second type emerges—green and leafless but with whorls of branchlike structures at nearly every node, making the stem look like a little Christmas tree.

Control Measures

Wherever found: Field horsetail is a strong competitor so try to improve soil structure and drainage. Practice clean cultivation and fertilize desirable plants to eventually drive out the horsetail. Dig out as many roots as possible. Most herbicides, even glyphosate, are ineffective in controlling it. Use dichlobenil (Ortho Casoron® Granules) beneath plants listed on the label to prevent spore germination as the late spring stalks die. Then place bark mulch over the treated area to maximize control.

HORSEWEED

Conyza canadensis,
syn. *Erigeron canadensis*
(Fleabane, marestail,
bitterweed)

As widespread as any weed in the United States, this annual has so little personality that it is seldom recognized until late summer when it flowers. Earlier in the year shallow-rooted

horseweed stays close to the ground as a rosette of dark green lance- or paddle-shaped leaves with or without a toothed margin. It can invade lawns and garden beds, preferring dry soil.

The Weed

Leaves appear randomly on the stem as it elongates. They become smaller near the top. Stems and leaves both have sparse coarse white bristles. When leaves are crushed a bitter oil gives them a pungent odor. The tall wandlike flower stems develop a large fluffy brush with a hundred or more little flower heads. Like miniature daisies each one has inconspicuous lavender to greenish white petals and yellow centers. These continue blooming until late fall, releasing thousands of seeds that float away on white bristles.

Control Measures

In lawns: Horseweed rosettes can easily be eliminated with a combination of 2,4-D and dicamba. A combination of 2,4-D and MCPP (Ortho Weed-B-Gon® Lawn Weed Killer for large areas; Ortho Weed-B-Gon® Jet Weeder—Formula II for spot treatment) is slightly less effective but does provide control. Available preemergent herbicides are not effective on this weed.

In gardens and around woody ornamentals: Cultivate early to destroy seedlings, then mulch to prevent the appearance of more weeds. Hand-pulling horseweed plants is easy and effective.

Horseweed is so nondescript that it often escapes notice until it is in bloom or until fluffy seed heads form.

JAPANESE HONEYSUCKLE

Lonicera japonica
(Honeysuckle)

A high-twining or trailing Asian vine that behaves itself where it is native, Japanese honeysuckle is a rampant weed in North America. Where it has escaped from cultivation—from New England to Lake Michigan and Texas—Japanese honeysuckle grows so vigorously that it carpets the ground, smothers shrubs, and strangles young trees. It grows most vigorously in fertile soil and full sunlight, producing abundant flowers and fruit. In shade and poor soil it may not flower and is less aggressive.

The Weed

The plant is evergreen, semievergreen, or deciduous depending on the climate. Dark green leaves are opposite each other. They usually have smooth edges but are sometimes toothed or deeply lobed. When this plant trails on the ground, roots develop at the leaf nodes. Underground stems also send up new shoots, and new plants come from seeds dropped by birds that eat the ¼-inch-long black berries, which form during the fall.

The marvelously fragrant, two-lipped tubular flowers occurring in pairs are white fading to yellow.

Control Measures

In lawns: If it has edged into the lawn, keep the grass constantly mowed to discourage the weed. Spray mature foliage with triclopyr (Ortho Poison Ivy & Poison Oak Killer—Formula II).

Around woody ornamentals: Where honeysuckle climbs up trees and shrubs, cut off and pull away the vines. Then treat the stump with triclopyr (Ortho Brush-B-Gon® Brush Killer,

Although Japanese honeysuckle is loved for its sweet-perfumed flowers, it can quickly cover other garden plants with its thick vines.

Ortho Poison Ivy & Poison Oak Killer—Formula II). Repeat as needed.

Foliage can also be sprayed with glyphosate if honeysuckle vines are not near desirable plants. Apply to foliage of existing vines and to foliage that resprouts from cut stubs. This treatment is most effective when applied to fully developed leaves. It can be used from summer up to and within two days after the first frost. Where honeysuckle leaves remain green they can be effectively sprayed right up until December. Thorough coverage is important but be sure the spray does not contact the foliage or green bark of desirable garden plants.

JERUSALEM ARTICHOKE

Helianthus tuberosus
(Girasole, earth-apple,
sunroot)

This North American native is valued for its ½- to 4-foot-long rhizomes that end in edible crunchy tubers. Cultivated by early Indians and now commercially raised and marketed as a food, Jerusalem artichoke grows so aggressively that when the plant escapes or tubers are left behind, it can rapidly become an extremely competitive and hard-to-eradicate weed.

All the live tubers left over winter sprout in late spring

from as deep as 12 inches in the soil. Jerusalem artichoke can produce great quantities of storage tubers—without competition one plant can form over 200 tubers in a growing season. The plant requires cross-pollination to form seeds; few are produced and most patches originate from a single tuber.

The Weed

The rough stems grow 2 to 12 feet tall and branch near the top. Leaves are bristly egg- or lance-shaped and the bright yellow blossoms

A native American plant, Jerusalem artichoke has edible tuberous roots. Eating them is one way to eradicate the plant.

resemble small sunflowers. They bloom as days become shorter in summer. New tubers form in early summer just before flowering starts.

Control Measures

In gardens: Dig up—and eat—existing tubers. Discourage more from forming by keeping shoots constantly cut, starting as soon as the first ones appear. Doing this for a growing season can reduce an infestation drastically. Use 2,4-D, dicamba, or glyphosate in nonfood gardens; however, the response is only fair. Herbicides provide best control if applied when shoots are 6 to 8 inches high. Repeat as needed on regrowth, especially during the vulnerable period in late spring if the situation seems to require the treatment. (Do not eat tubers of sprayed Jerusalem artichoke plants.)

Jimsonweed's large, funnel-shaped flowers make it easy to identify. All parts of the plant are poisonous.

JIMSONWEED

Datura stramonium
(Jamestown weed, thornapple, stinkweed, mad-apple, devils trumpet, apple of Peru)

An ill-scented and dangerously poisonous annual, jimsonweed reproduces only by seed. Its bruised leaves and stems give off a sickening odor. No part of jimsonweed should ever be eaten, as its alkaloids can be lethal. The weed occurs worldwide in yards, fields, and vacant lots.

The Weed

Growing 1 to 4 feet tall, the plant looks something like a small tree with a smooth stout stem, wide-spreading branches, and large smooth dark green leaves rather like those of an oak. Beautiful, 3- to 4-inch-long, white or purple trumpet-shaped flowers develop in crotches of the forking branches. They bloom all summer and into fall. Seedpods are large, globular, and usually spiny.

Control Measures

In gardens: A few swipes with a sharp hoe or hand-pulling is effective if done before seeds have matured; wear gloves for protection. Jimsonweed does not respond to most available herbicides. Glyphosate kills it but may be difficult to apply without harming nearby desirable plants.

JOHNSONGRASS

Sorghum halepense
(Egyptiangrass, St. Mary's grass, false guineagrass, Cubagrass, Morocco millet, Aleppo grass, milletgrass, maidencane, meansgrass)

This grass was introduced to the United States from the Mediterranean during the mid-1800s for pasture forage and hay. Its aggressive spreading habit and deep root system resulted in runaway weediness. It is one of the most serious weeds in cultivated fields, in waste places, and along roadsides in much of the Southwest.

Johnsongrass seasonally produces three different kinds of rootstocks that grow to depths varying partly with cultural treatment. Big ones break up when the ground is cultivated deeply, and every segment with a node can produce one or more new stalks.

The Weed

This coarse warm-season perennial grass, growing to 6 feet tall, spreads by seeds and extensive freely branching rhizomes, which develop mainly after flowering. Johnsongrass is easily identified by the presence of these thick scaly sharp-pointed rhizomes and the brittle whitish midvein of its long smooth leaves. The distinguishing midvein is apparent even on seedlings. Unlike quackgrass (see page 80), there are no auricles (earlike projections) at the base of the leaf blade. The big

loose flowering head with whorls of branches is almost wine-colored.

Control Measures

In lawns: Johnsongrass does not tolerate constant mowing; weekly mowing will usually eliminate it.

In gardens: Rhizomes start to grow when the soil temperature reaches 60° F. Apply a preemergent treatment of benefin, DCPA (Dacthal®—Ortho Garden Weed Preventer), or trifluralin well before the soil temperature reaches 70° F. This will prevent germination of seeds, which can remain dormant for many years. On existing plants spot-spray with glyphosate (Ortho Kleenup® Grass & Weed Killer, Ortho Kleenup® Spot Weed & Grass Killer) after plants are 18 inches tall or before seed heads form. This produces faster and more effective control of rhizomes than hand-pulling or hoeing.

In cold-winter areas plowing or deep cultivation in

Look for the whitish leaf midrib to identify Johnsongrass, a spreading perennial that grows to 6 feet tall.

fall exposes rhizomes to frost and can improve control of established weed stands.

Around woody ornamentals: Spray fluazifop-butyl (Ortho Grass-B-Gon® Grass Killer) on unmowed Johnsongrass growing with plants listed on the label. A second application may be needed to control mature Johnsongrass.

KNAWEL

Scleranthus annuus
(German knotgrass,
German moss)

This tough little cool-season or winter annual is a persistent weed in gravelly or sandy soils that are dry. In lawns it grows only 3 to 4 inches tall, but in gardens or unmowed areas it forms mats or sprawling clumps a foot or more wide. Looking much like grass, knawel may not be noticed at first.

The Weed

Narrow, sharp-pointed, awl-shaped leaves bend downward and are opposite each other on the spreading much-branched stems. Clusters of small green flowers form spiny burs in the leaf axils (angle formed by leaf and stem) from spring until fall, liberating minute seeds that are extraordinarily viable and may lie dormant for several years before germinating.

Control Measures

In lawns: Knawel can be controlled by a combination of 2,4-D and dicamba applied in mid- to late fall but not by 2,4-D alone. Heavy infestations can be spot-treated with

Look closely to identify knawel and eradicate it before it can form seeds. Once seeds fall, they will continue to germinate for many years.

glyphosate (Ortho Kleenup® Spot Weed & Grass Killer) and then reseeded. Attempts should be made to improve growing conditions by fertilizing or incorporating organic

matter if the lawn is being renovated.

In gardens and around woody ornamentals: The weed is easily discouraged by early and clean cultivation. Mulching maintains control. Application of glyphosate plus oxyfluorfen (Ortho Kleenup® Super Edger) kills existing weeds and prevents more weeds from appearing for up to three months.

KNOTWEED, JAPANESE

Polygonum cuspidatum
(Japanese or Mexican bamboo, wild rhubarb)

Japanese knotweed grows almost anywhere, persisting even in rough places where little else can thrive. It overwhelms all other vegetation. Its jointed woody stems resemble bamboo and it grows with the same amazing speed, hence its common name. Its leaves are heart-shaped, not at all like bamboo, which is a huge grass.

Reproduction is almost entirely by stout rhizomes, which grow as deep as 5 feet. The grooved stems are killed by the first light frost but the foliage is held until late fall; reddish brown dead stalks remain standing over winter.

The Weed

The large heart-shaped leaves taper to a slender tip. Great arching stems, which can reach as high as 9 feet, begin as pointed green spears spotted red and with leaves still rolled around them. At this stage the stems can be cut like those of rhubarb, a relative, and cooked with sugar to make pies. Left untouched the shoots grow with almost frightening speed from underground stems with large food reserves. By late summer some of the plants have clouds of delicate, creamy male flowers. Other plants bear plainer, drooping female flowers that produce papery three-winged seeds. For an

Japanese knotweed sends up many shoots from deep, sturdy rootstocks. Its jointed appearance and quick growth have earned it another common name: Japanese bamboo.

unknown reason the seedlings die within a few weeks after they germinate.

Sakhalin knotweed (*P. sachalinense*) is even more robust but not seen as frequently. Its leaves don't taper to a point and its flowers are greenish instead of whitish. Otherwise it is quite similar.

Control Measures

In lawns: A two- to four-year program of removing all young shoots may eventually exhaust food reserves. Using dicamba on lawn grasses listed on the label will shorten the time for control.

In gardens and around woody ornamentals: Unless repeated continually hoeing or cutting shoots off only encourages new and more profuse growth. Shoots can push right through asphalt so mulching isn't the answer. Try spot-treatment with glyphosate (Ortho Kleenup® Systemic Weed & Grass Killer) when knotweed is growing actively and has reached the bud to early flowering stage. Triclopyr (Ortho Poison Ivy & Poison Oak Killer) can also be used; take care to keep the herbicide away from areas where roots of desirable plants might absorb it.

KNOTWEED, PROSTRATE

Polygonum aviculare
(Knotgrass, doorweed, matgrass, yardweed)

The first weed to appear in spring, prostrate knotweed occurs most often in soils of low fertility and so solidified by foot or wheel traffic that other plants cannot grow there. Seedlings of this annual weed sprout in compacted places, bare spots in lawns, and cracks in pavement. At first knotweed seedlings look very much like grass seedlings, especially if they have germinated thickly, but their stems have a red base and are quite different. These seedlings soon branch out from the wiry taproot and spread along the ground without rooting further. By midsummer dense mats, which can reach 2 feet across, crowd out turfgrasses and desirable garden plants.

The Weed

The bluish green oval leaves are about 1 inch long and ¼ inch wide; they are attached to the creeping stems at swollen joints. From summer to fall small white to pinkish flowers form inside a thin papery sheath in the leaf axils (angle formed by leaf and stem). Depending on where it is located, knotweed can be very compact or the branches can be long and slender with more space between the nobby nodes (leaf bases).

Control Measures

In lawns: Promote turf growth by reducing traffic in the area, fertilizing, liming (if necessary), and mowing no shorter than 1½ inches. Pre-emergent treatment with benefin controls seedlings. For emerged knotweed, apply a combination of 2,4-D and MCPP (Ortho Weed-B-Gon® Lawn Weed Killer) or 2,4-D and dicamba (Ortho Chickweed, Spurge & Oxalis Killer D) early because it becomes more difficult to control late

Prostrate knotweed survives on hard-beaten paths and in cracks in the pavement, and it spreads to nearby lawns and gardens.

in the season. Spot application of glyphosate (Ortho Kleenup® Spot Weed & Grass Killer) can be used to kill individual plants.

In gardens: A preemergent treatment of trifluralin can be applied according to label restrictions. Shallow hoeing or other cultivation destroys seedlings and mature knotweed. Hand-pulling mature weeds is easy. Mulching with an organic material keeps weeds out and also improves the soil.

In walks, driveways, patios, etc.: To eliminate knotweed growing in paving cracks and similar situations, pulling with a twist of the hand is easy. The weeds can be spot-treated with glyphosate plus acifluorfen (Ortho Kleenup® Grass & Weed Killer) to maintain control for the rest of the season. In driveways and other larger areas, the soil sterilant prometon (Ortho Triox® Vegetation Killer) provides year-long control but should never be applied where roots from trees or shrubs might absorb it. In this situation use glyphosate plus oxyfluorfen (Ortho Kleenup® Super Edger.)

KUDZU

Pueraria lobata
(Kudzu-vine)

A fearsome perennial trailing or high-climbing vine, kudzu climbs over and onto everything within reach of its vigorous 10-foot-long runners. Blanketing roadsides and woodland edges in the south-

eastern United States west to Texas and now occurring north to Pennsylvania and New Jersey, this pest can grow up to 60 feet a year. Kudzu can kill the trees and shrubs it covers. It was originally planted as a forage crop or to control erosion but escaped to become an aggressive weed. Birds spread the seeds.

The Weed
The heavy twining stems are hairy and may become woody. They bear large three-leaflet leaves that are smooth and irregularly lobed. By late summer and early fall showy, reddish or bluish purple pea-like flowers bloom. These have the fragrance of grapes. Seeds resembling mottled beans form in papery seedpods and are covered with

Kudzu is so rampant that it buries whole landscapes. To avoid this fate learn to recognize its leaves while it is young.

short reddish hairs. The roots, which send up new shoots, are really tubers.

Control Measures
Wherever found: Herbicides work best when applied in late summer through early

fall—after full leaf expansion and before autumn leaf drop—to actively growing vines. Triclopyr (Ortho Brush-B-Gon® Brush Killer) works well as a foliar spray as does glyphosate when applied two to three weeks after bloom. The herbicide 2,4-D is fairly effective but not as much as the other two.

Try to control kudzu early before it engulfs desirable plants. Once entangled with a tree or shrub, it is difficult to get the vines down without breaking the limbs of the supporting plants. Where kudzu climbs on trees and shrubs, cut off the vines at ground level—pull down tops if possible—and apply triclopyr (Ortho Brush-B-Gon® Brush Killer) to the vine's cut stubs.

LADYSTHUMB

Polygonum persicaria
(Spotted smartweed, persicary, redshank, redweed, heartweed)

A prolific summer annual, ladysthumb reproduces only by seeds. Preferring moist

places but tolerating dry ones, this fast-growing weed occurs in gardens, landscaped areas, and cracks in walkways. Seeds lie dormant over winter, germinating in spring. They are a source of food for wildlife, but a nuisance to gardeners. The weed's juices, like the juices of other smartweeds, can cause an uncomfortable smarting or stinging pain.

The Weed
Ladysthumb leaves are long and tapering and usually have a reddish, brownish, or purplish triangular mark near the middle. Upright stems grow from a short taproot and are green or reddish. These are smooth except for the distinct nodes, or leaf bases.

From midsummer until frost, ladysthumb and other smartweeds produce beady little flowers tightly crowded onto narrow spikes at the ends of stems and branches. The 1-inch-long spikes of ladysthumb are pink.

Ladysthumb and Pennsylvania smartweed (*P. pensylvanicum*) have similar appearances and growth

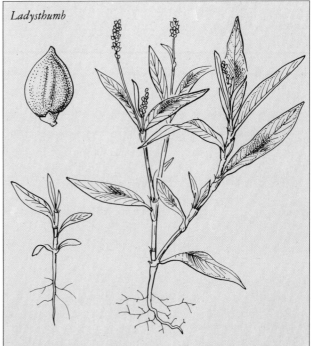

Ladysthumb

This annual weed produces narrow spikes of beady pink flowers from mid-summer until frost. Seeds (top left) lie dormant over winter and germinate in spring. Seedlings (bottom left) often appear in cracks in walkways as well as in garden beds.

habits, however since controls are the same telling them apart isn't critical.

Control Measures

In lawns: Ladysthumb can be a problem in poorly maintained lawns. This and other smartweeds respond well to a postemergent application of 2,4-D and MCPP (Ortho Weed-B-Gon® Lawn Weed Killer).

In gardens and around woody ornamentals: Spot-treat around nonfood crop plants with glyphosate (Ortho Kleenup® Grass & Weed Killer, Ortho Kleenup® Spot Weed & Grass Killer). Ladysthumb is easily controlled by early cultivation;

Ladysthumb shows the typical papery sheath that forms at leaf bases of plants in the genus Polygonum.

don't allow it to flower or form seeds. Because the weed often grows in acid soil, liming may help. Maintaining a mulch is an effective preventive. Hand-pulling works only if the soil is moist so that the brittle roots come out entirely.

LAMBSQUARTERS

Chenopodium album
(Fat hen, white pigweed, white goosefoot)

This early germinating summer annual is familiar to most gardeners despite being extremely variable in size, branching, leaf shape, and flowering characteristics. It

Early Europeans used lambsquarters in cooking much as we now use its close relative spinach.

is one of the most common weed pests in gardens throughout the United States. Lambsquarters may appear in new turf growing on former cropland, but does not usually persist. Its pollen may irritate some hayfever sufferers and it is a host plant for beet leafhoppers, which transmit curlytop virus.

The Weed

From its short branched taproot come upright, grooved stems often streaked with red or light green. The stalked leaves tend to be broadly triangular, becoming smaller toward the top of the plant. Leaves are shallowly toothed and have a white powdery covering that is especially noticeable on new foliage. Loose clusters of little green ball-like flowers develop from the leaf axils (angle formed where leaf meets stem) whether the plant has grown to its full height of 5 to 6 feet, or has been mowed back to only a few inches. From early summer to early fall an average-sized specimen can produce several hundred shining black seeds that can lie dormant in the soil for years.

Control Measures

In lawns: Spray with MCPP (Ortho Chickweed & Clover Control) or a mixture of 2,4-D and MCPP (Ortho Weed-B-Gon® Lawn Weed Killer) in spring if the weed is a problem. Follow good management practices to keep turf vigorous.

In gardens: A common nuisance, lambsquarters can be readily prevented by a pre-emergent application of DCPA (Dacthal®—Ortho Garden Weed Preventer) or trifluralin. Seeds can germinate throughout the growing season. Spot-treat in flower gardens with glyphosate (Ortho Kleenup® Spot Weed & Grass Killer) or glyphosate combined with acifluorfen (Ortho Kleenup® Grass & Weed Killer). Mulching, regular cultivation, or hand-pulling will control seedlings.

Around woody ornamentals: Treat as suggested for gardens. A permanent mulch of organic or synthetic material will eliminate lambsquarters and many other weeds.

LESPEDEZA, COMMON AND KOREAN

Lespedeza striata and *L. stipulacea*
(Japanese and Korean clover)

These small annual weeds suddenly become noticeable in lawns in mid- or late summer, even though they germinate in late spring. They grow so close to the ground that mowers barely trim them. Branching wider and wider as the summer progresses, their matted growth chokes out thin turf. Neither one is particular about soil type. Common lespedeza is found increasingly in southern lawns.

The Weed

The dark green leaves are three-parted like those of clover and have conspicuous straight veins. The wiry stems come only from a tough taproot. By late summer and continuing until late fall, pinkish or purplish flowers that resemble tiny sweet peas peep from leaf axils of common lespedeza. Flowers of Korean lespedeza cluster at the tips of all branches.

Control Measures

In lawns: Lespedeza is difficult to control. A pre-emergent application of bensulide or DCPA (Dacthal®) gives only poor control. When lespedeza is growing actively and is not under drought stress, 2,4-D combined with MCPP (Ortho Weed-B-Gon® Jet Weeder—Formula II) or 2,4-D combined with dicamba (Ortho Chickweed, Spurge & Oxalis Killer D) control it with repeat applications.

Repeated applications of methanearsonates also control the weed. These herbicides work best on young weeds. If dense patches are to be killed and the bare spots reseeded, glyphosate can be used. Fertilize well and follow recommended practices to thicken turf and crowd out weeds.

In gardens and around woody ornamentals: Light cultivation and mulching will control lespedeza, which is shallow rooted.

Cloverlike with small pink or purple flowers resembling sweet peas, lespedeza is a sneaky lawn invader.

LIPPIA

Phyla nodiflora, syn.
Lippia nodiflora
(Matchweed, matgrass,
creeping-charlie,
frogfruit)

An aggressive perennial in
southern states from Florida
to Texas and up into Ar-
kansas, lippia is grown in hot,
dry climates as a ground
cover or lawn substitute that
needs no irrigation. It is a
weed in grass lawns, where it
forms smothering mats.
Lippia has wiry stems up to 3
feet long that creep close to
the ground. Where nodes
touch the soil they root, forming large patches.

The Weed
The wedge-shaped leaves
have rounded tips and
toothed margins and are
opposite each other on the

*Improving a lawn's growing
conditions makes lippia less
likely to invade or survive as
a turf weed.*

stems. Mats send up many
curious, dark red flower buds
that look like the heads of
kitchen matches. Later these
are ringed with small pink to
white flowers.

Control Measures
In lawns: Lippia is found most
often in thin turf. Improve
turf density with good
management, including feeding as recommended by soil
analysis, and proper mowing
and irrigation. Increase acidity
with a sulfur compound if the
soil is extremely alkaline.
Eliminate lippia patches early
with a combination of 2,4-D

*Hundreds of mallow seedlings, each with two heart-shaped leaves,
will cover the ground where a mallow plant has scattered seeds.*

and MCPP (Ortho Weed-B-
Gon® Lawn Weed Killer) or
2,4-D combined with
dicamba on listed turfgrasses.
   In gardens and around
woody ornamentals: Raise
runners with a shallow
cultivating tool and hand-pull
or grub out entire plants.
Around flowers and woody
ornamentals, eliminate with
a combination of glyphosate
and oxyfluorfen (Ortho
Kleenup® Super Edger)
according to label directions.

MALLOW

Malva neglecta, syn.
·M. rotundifolia
(Cheeseweed, musk plant,
low mallow)

Although this weed re-
produces only from seeds,
mallow's spreading top and
deep taproot both branch
freely. It grows close to the
ground, or to several feet in
height. This attractive plant
was introduced to North
America as an ornamental but
escaped to become a pest.
Rarely a serious problem, mallow flourishes in infertile soil,
invading lawns, lots, and landscaped areas throughout the
United States.

The Weed
Variable in height and spread,
mallow may develop as a very
leafy annual, biennial, or
perennial, depending upon the
climate. Leaves are round or
kidney-shaped, slightly lobed,
and toothed. About the size

of a silver dollar, the leaves
grow on long stalks, making
them easy to identify. Small,
pale pink to lavender flowers
appear from late spring until
late fall. Tips of the five
flower petals are blunt and
notched. Dark brown seeds
develop in a flattened disk
that breaks into sections like
a cake or wheel of cheese that
has been cut; one seed forms
in each flat-sided section.

Control Measures
In lawns: Control mallow with
a combination of 2,4-D and
MCPP (Ortho Weed-B-Gon®
Lawn Weed Killer) or with
a combination of 2,4-D,
MCPP, and dicamba for su-
perior control (Ortho Chickweed, Spurge & Oxalis Killer
D). Apply while weeds are
small and before they begin
to spread out and interfere
with turf growth. To prevent
mallow in new lawns follow
cultural practices that promote vigorous turf growth.
   In gardens: Hoe or cultivate seedlings as they appear. (The leaves of mallow
seedlings look like those of
young hollyhocks but are
smooth or slightly fuzzy, not
hairy.) Mulching will keep
seedlings from emerging.
   Around woody
ornamentals: Spot-treat with
glyphosate (Ortho Kleenup®
Systemic Weed & Grass
Killer) or cut tops off below
the root crown with shallow
hoeing. Mulch to prevent
reemergence.

MAYWEED

Anthemis cotula
(Dogfennel, wild chamomile,
stinking daisy, manzanillo)

Bruising the stems of the lacy-
leafed mayweed releases a
disagreeable odor, and the
juice of this weed can cause
blisters. Mayweed has a short
taproot and usually grows in
masses, but it is not a serious
pest, occurring mostly in
waste places.

The Weed
Mayweed is an annual that
germinates in spring, blooms
and forms seeds from late
spring through late summer
or early fall, and dies with the

*Although it resembles its relative
the tea herb chamomile, mayweed has an unpleasant odor
and its juice may cause skin
irritation.*

frost in cold-winter climates.
In warm-winter climates, the
weed also germinates in fall
and grows through the winter
as a winter annual.
   The upright stems can
grow to 2 feet tall. Small
daisylike flower heads are
borne at the ends of the
branches. Stems below the
flowers have fine hairs.
   Corn chamomile (*A.
arvensis*) is almost identical to
mayweed but lacks the odor
and acid juice. Pineappleweed
(*Matricaria matricarioides*) has
similar ferny leaves but a
pleasant pineapple odor when
crushed, and its flowers lack
showy petals.

Control Measures
In lawns: If desired, apply 2,4-
D; however, repeated mowing
discourages the weed.

In gardens: Spot-treat in flower beds with glyphosate (Ortho Kleenup® Systemic Weed & Grass Killer). Clean cultivation started early keeps mayweed from becoming established and forming seeds for the next year. Wear gloves if hand-pulling. Mulching prevents seedlings from becoming a problem. Mow any colonies in nearby waste places to prevent an invasion.

Around woody ornamentals: Control as in gardens or with a combination of glyphosate and oxyfluorfen (Ortho Kleenup® Super Edger).

MILKWEED

Asclepias syriaca
(Silkweed, cottonweed)

A tall, perennial wildflower in loamy soils along roadsides, in ditches, or in pastures, milkweed can find its way into gardens because its seeds are airborne. Milkweed often grows in thick patches propagated from buds on its long horizontal rootstock. Seedlings are able to reproduce new plants from their roots three weeks after emergence. In midspring shoots begin poking up from old roots, which can grow as deep as 12 feet in some soils.

The Weed
Milkweed has a single tall stem that doesn't often form branches. All parts of the plant have milky white sap. In early summer clusters of pinkish flowers develop near the top in the axils (angle formed by leaf and stem) of the large oval leaves. Only one or two large, soft, and warty pods develop from a cluster, but each one is filled with many neatly layered flat seeds adorned with beautiful silky hairs. In early fall the pods mature and release the round brown seeds. These float away on water or in the air, buoyed by their long hairs.

Milkweed flowers are pink and fragrant, but they must not be allowed to form seedpods or the airborne seeds will spread the infestation further.

Control Measures
In lawns: Regular mowing slowly reduces established colonies.

In gardens: Keep tops continuously chopped off by hoeing, rather than trying to grub out the spreading rhizomes. Cultivate every two or three weeks if seedlings are noticed. Prevent seed production and establishment in nearby fields (and dispersal to lawns and gardens) with glyphosate. Application during the bud to bloom stage gives the best results.

MINER'S LETTUCE

Montia perfoliata
(Indian or Spanish lettuce)

This curious fleshy annual has become a common weed in gardens, orchards, and vineyards on the West Coast. It is especially troublesome in California, where it is native.

Miner's lettuce was so named by 49ers in California's gold country because it was a wild food gathered by prospectors.

The Weed
Seedling and mature basal leaves are long and narrow. Farther up the 4- to 12-inch stems are semi-circular leaves united at the base to form a disk or broad funnel through which the stem appears to project. The leaves are edible. Numerous small, light pink or white, five-petalled flowers emerge from just above these funnels. These produce seedpods containing a great many small, shiny black seeds.

Control Measures
In gardens and around woody ornamentals: Regular cultivation or mulching is the only control needed.

MISTLETOE

Phoradendron flavescens
var. *macrophyllum*
(American mistletoe)

Long associated with Christmas celebrations, these woody semiparasites have become an increasingly common pest. They attach themselves to shade trees (particularly Modesto and Arizona ash) in California and several southwestern states, seriously weakening or even killing the host by stealing nutrients and moisture. The evergreen mistletoe balls look very strange after tree leaves have fallen. There may be a few or many such clumps growing on a single tree.

Cedar waxwings and other birds spread the seeds after they feed on the sticky white mistletoe berries. Birds may also carry the seeds from one tree to another on beaks or feet. Workers pruning trees may accidentally spread the sticky seeds too. When conditions are favorable, the seeds, which adhere to tree bark, send rootlike structures into the tree.

The Weed
There are 100 species of American mistletoe, eight of them occurring in California. The yellowish green leaves are thick, firm, and nearly oval. Stems are jointed, and the tiny flowers are often clustered in whorls on spikes. Dense mistletoe plants may eventually grow to be several feet in diameter.

Control Measures
On woody ornamentals: Infested limbs can be pruned out every year but it is hard to find all the small young mistletoe plants. A foam-type formulation of 2,4-D combined with dicamba is registered for use in California, and should be applied to cut mistletoe stubs during the dormant season, after the leaves of the host tree drop and before new leaves appear in spring. In new residential

Mistletoe may signify romance at Christmas, but the plant seems less romantic when sapping the strength of a favorite shade tree.

areas, plant resistant trees, such as Chinese pistache, eucalyptus, sweet gum, London plane, or ginkgo.

MONEYWORT

Lysimachia nummularia
(Creeping-charlie, creeping-jenny, creeping-loosestrife)

Some would argue that this plant is a pretty ground cover, but it is more often a troublesome pest, invading lawns and forming dense mats. No other plant looks quite like it. The stems of this invasive, creeping perennial root in every direction, creating patches in lawns, gardens, and other landscaped areas. It grows best in moist shade but tolerates sun.

Some gardeners use moneywort as a ground cover, but its overexuberant spreading habit can turn it into a weed if it isn't planted with caution.

The Weed
The smooth, creeping stems branch freely, spreading 2 feet wide. Pairs of glossy, stemless leaves are nearly as round as small coins, hence the name of the weed. Bright yellow flowers with five broad lobes shine from the dark green foliage throughout the summer.

Control Measures
In lawns: Moneywort is readily controlled by 2,4-D. Another method of control is to raise the weed's runners by raking and then mowing close. Improve drainage if necessary. Fertilize to help turf grow vigorously.

In gardens: Rake out and destroy weeds by shallow cultivation.

Around woody ornamentals: Keep weeds smothered with a landscape fabric mulch. Spot-spray with glyphosate (Ortho Kleenup® Spot Weed & Grass Killer).

MORNING-GLORY, TALL AND IVYLEAF

Ipomoea purpurea and *I. hederacea*

These two morningglories are slender annual vines with beautiful flowers and slightly hairy stems that twine around anything nearby. Sometimes perennial or biennial depending upon the climate, they can choke or smother the plants they grow on. Cultivated varieties of morningglory are less troublesome, but can be weedy if they reseed where they aren't wanted.

The Weed
Tall morningglory has heart-shaped leaves and large, attractive, flaring blooms. The blooms are blue, purple, red, white, or multicolored. Leaves of ivyleaf morningglory have three distinct lobes. Its funnel-shaped flowers are sky blue at first, turning purplish as they age. Both species bloom from early summer until frost and reproduce profusely from seed. The seeds form in bristly seedpods that can be carried on clothing and animal fur to start infestations elsewhere.

Control Measures
In lawns: The weed is sometimes introduced with topsoil or is already present in new lawns that were formerly farmland. Spray the lawn with 2,4-D (Ortho Weed-B-Gon® Lawn Weed Killer, Ortho Chickweed, Spurge & Oxalis Killer D).

These tall morningglory vines are competing with the corn plants for nutrients and light.

In gardens and around woody ornamentals: Cultivate soil to keep seedlings from developing. Mulching prevents their appearance. Hand-pull any that escape when they are small before they flower and develop seeds.

MOSS

Polytrichum and other genera

Although moss is beautiful in a forest or Japanese garden, it indicates trouble when it invades a lawn. The presence of moss usually means an acid soil that is often wet or compacted, and starved turf. Peat and spaghnum mosses are useful to gardeners, but not these weedy mosses.

The Weed
Mosses are very dwarf, leafy plants with threadlike branching or simple stems forming

Moss can invade a lawn when soil conditions are unfavorable for grasses: acidic, compacted, or infertile.

mats on moist ground. Like ferns they have no flowers and reproduce by spores or from buds.

Control Measures
In lawns: Have a complete soil analysis done or consult your county extension service for recommendations on developing healthier turf. See whether drainage should be improved by aerating the lawn. Pruning nearby trees may help, since shade and poor air circulation foster moss growth. Avoid overwatering. Existing moss

can be killed with copper sulfate, iron (ferric) sulfate, or a fatty acid-based product labeled for that use.

MUGWORT

Artemisia vulgaris (Chrysanthemum weed, wormwood)

The chrysanthemumlike leaves of this invasive perennial fool many gardeners until the chrysanthemum flowers fail to appear. The white, woolly leaf undersides, the lack of showy flowers, and an odor like sage rather than chrysanthemum confirm the disappointing deception. Some reproduction is from seeds, but the weed mostly spreads by its extensive roots. Many nurseries are heavily infested with this pest, and it can spread to your garden on the rootballs of their stock. Once transplanted, mugwort's forking, horizontal rhizomes spread rapidly in the garden and even move into lawns where the weed tolerates mowing. Mugwort is related to western sagebrush.

The Weed
Stems can grow 3 to 6 feet tall. Leaves are aromatic when crushed and 2 to 6 inches long, resembling chrysanthemum leaves. When mugwort is not mowed, inconspicuous flowers in leafy spikes appear from midsummer onward.

Control Measures
In lawns: Mugwort is difficult to control. Spray with 2,4-D combined with MCPP or with dicamba, repeating the treatment each time regrowth appears.

In gardens: Hand-weeding is not very effective, since any pieces of the rhizome left in the soil will resprout. Remove as much of the root as possible, repeating the attempt as new shoots appear. Where safety of other plants permits,

The woolly white leaf undersides of mugwort distinguish it from garden chrysanthemum, which it resembles.

spot-treat carefully with glyphosate before the weed begins to bloom.

Around woody ornamentals: Apply dichlobenil between late fall and very early spring to prevent germination, or spot-treat patches with glyphosate (Ortho Kleenup® Super Edger). Examine rootballs of nursery stock carefully for mugwort shoots or roots and avoid bringing infested plant material into the garden.

MULTIFLORA ROSE

Rosa multiflora
(Wild rose)

A very vigorous, pest-free woody shrub, multiflora rose grows 10 to 15 feet wide and about as tall. Commonly used as a rootstock on which ornamental roses are grafted, as a wildlife cover, as erosion control ground cover, and formerly recommended as a living fence, it is also a weedy nuisance around the yard and garden. The seeds germinate readily and are often spread in bird droppings. The rapidly spreading habit of this weed and its adaptability to a variety of conditions have resulted in such uncontrolled multiplication that growing or selling multifora roses is now prohibited in many states. The weed is not a problem in areas that are cultivated annually, but it can get firmly established in landscaped and unmaintained areas.

The Weed

The long, thorny green stems grow upright at first, but tips droop to the ground and root there, forming larger clumps. The leaves have 5 to 11 (usually 9) leaflets. Small, fragrant blossoms about the size of raspberry or blackberry flowers appear in late spring in clusters of 25 to 100. Each flower has five white to pinkish petals. Small rose hips mature through the summer and early fall. They turn red and remain on the plant until spring or until eaten by birds.

Birds often drop seeds of multiflora rose, an aggressive rose species that can overrun garden areas not cultivated annually.

Control Measures

Wherever found: In open fields and recreation areas, control multiflora roses with a combination of mowing and herbicide treatment. Repeated foliar sprays of triclopyr (Ortho Brush-B-Gon® Brush Killer), 2,4-D plus dicamba, or glyphosate applied to actively growing plants are effective. Use 2,4-D to kill small seedlings. In large areas, bulldoze or consult a licensed pesticide operator who is permitted to use additional, suitable herbicides.

NIGHTSHADE

Solanum dulcamara
(European bittersweet, bitter nightshade, climbing nightshade)
S. nigrum or *S. americanum*
(Black nightshade, deadly nightshade, poisonberry, garden nightshade)

The nightshade family is filled with contradictions: It includes members that are definitely food plants—tomato, potato, eggplant—and also members that are clearly weeds—horsenettle, jimsonweed, and many others. Some

Wherever the purple flowers and bright red berries of European bittersweet are visible, dig down to the roots and grub the viny weed entirely.

are known to be poisonous, particularly to grazing animals and, even, possibly to humans. If not actually deadly these nightshades can cause nausea or dizziness.

European bittersweet is a particular nuisance in areas seldom cultivated because it frequently twines through shrubbery. It is often spread by bird droppings. Black nightshade, more common in cultivated gardens, is less troublesome, competing in ordinary weedy ways.

The Weed

European bittersweet is a perennial; its vinelike, woody stems may grow 10 feet long but are often killed to the ground in cold winters. The slender, heart-shaped leaves are often slightly lobed at the base and resemble a mitten. Small, star-shaped purple flowers with a column of bright yellow anthers are rather attractive, as are the berries, which are bright red when ripe.

Black or American nightshade is a densely branching annual with softer, almost diamond-shaped leaves and little white flowers blooming from summer until fall. Its small berries turn almost black when they mature.

Control Measures

In gardens: Constant and shallow clean cultivation eliminates black nightshade, an annual, as a pest.

Around woody ornamentals: Grub out the shallow roots of European bittersweet, a perennial. Mulch heavily and watch carefully for any new seedlings to avoid reinfestation. Glyphosate plus oxyfluorfen (Ortho Kleenup® Super Edger) kills existing plants and prevents germination for up to three months.

NIMBLEWILL

Muhlenbergia schreberi
(Dropseed)

A native, warm-season perennial grass, nimblewill is an annoying nuisance even though it is only mildly aggressive. When the weed infests lawns, its gray-green summer color and tan winter color spoil the lawn's appearance. Pieces of stem often break off and start new colonies. The weed grows in sun or shade and infests gardens and lawns.

The Weed

Nimblewill has distinctly parallel-grooved leaves. The ½- to 2-inch long leaf blades are sharply angled from the stem and the edges are smooth. Nimblewill has delicate roots resembling thin wires, and its

A grass of a different color, nimblewill stands out in a lawn by being gray-green in summer and brown in winter.

slender stems sometimes root from swollen lower nodes (leaf bases). Plants sprawl outward, especially when mowed. Nimblewill can be confused with bermudagrass at first glance. However, bermudagrass has firm, scaly rootstocks, definite jointed runners, no grooves on it leaves, rough leaf margins, and spreading seed heads.

Nimbleweed is dormant from fall until early spring. Seeds and established plants begin to grow in spring.

Control Measures

In lawns: Rake matted stems upright and then mow close to reduce spreading. Attempts to cut patches out may leave bits to continue growth. If the situation is serious, spot-treat with glyphosate (Ortho Kleenup® Grass & Weed Killer) and reseed. Plan to do this in very late summer when nimblewill is still growing actively. Leave the weed unmowed a couple of weeks before spraying so there is enough foliage to absorb the spray. Figure on another week before reseeding the spot. Keep turf vigorous.

In gardens and around woody ornamentals: Nimblewill is easy to grub out and to eliminate with clean cultivation because its roots are shallow. It is not likely to invade mulched areas.

NUTSEDGE, YELLOW AND PURPLE

Cyperus esculentus and *C. rotundus*
(Nutgrass, cocosedge, cocograss, watergrass)

These similar weeds are notorious perennial pests in lawns and gardens, reproducing from underground nutlets

Hand-pulling nutsedge plants does not stop the weed. It grows back from small tubers that radiate from the central roots.

or tubers. When hand-weeded, the stems break off leaving behind the tubers, which readily sprout and grow new plants.

The Weed

With their crisp, grasslike leaves, nutsedges are often mistaken for grasses but are really sedges. Looking down on one shows that its shiny leaves point outward in three directions, not two as grass does. Stems are triangular and solid, not round and hollow like most grasses.

The difference underground is more important. Several slender white rhizomes (underground stems) radiate from the center of

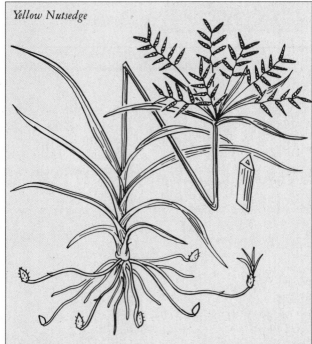

Yellow Nutsedge

Nutsedge is often mistaken for a grass but its stems (top right) are triangular, not rounded, in cross-section. Underground nutlets or tubers grow at the tips of the rhizomes. These quickly produce new plants if the main stem is broken off.

each plant. Chaffy, edible nutlets form at the tips of yellow nutsedge roots, mostly near the soil surface but sometimes deeper. Purple nutsedge tubers form chains and taste bitter. New plantlets grow from the tubers and can form large patches.

Uncontrolled nutsedge blooms in late summer to early fall. Most of the seeds, dormant at first, are able to germinate, especially in the top 1½ inches of soil. In cultivated ground, nutsedge spreads primarily by tuberous propagation. Tubers form quickly when days are short in early fall, and more slowly in spring and early summer. Shoots form most readily in summer when temperatures are high.

Control Measures

In lawns: Control nutsedge tops selectively with methanearsonates (Ortho Crabgrass & Nutgrass Killer) except in St. Augustine grass, carpetgrass, or centipedegrass lawns. Two treatments about a week apart are needed for good control.

In gardens: Cultivate early and frequently to induce seed germination. Then keep seedlings chopped off; they are easily destroyed by cultivation. In established infestations cutting apart rhizomes may stimulate formation of new plants, which are best controlled by constant cultivation. Remove any visible nutlets. If exposed, nutlets will deteriorate over the winter, so cultivate again in late fall.

In vegetable gardens use a mulch made of landscape fabric rather than plastic. The fabric is more resistant to penetration by the tough nut-sedge shoots.

Around woody ornamentals: Spray emerged nutsedge with glyphosate (Ortho Kleenup® Systemic Weed & Grass Killer), and re-peat if new sprouts appear. Use a fabric mulch or apply dichlobenil (Ortho Casoron® Granules) to prevent seed germination between late fall and early spring.

ORCHARDGRASS

Dactylis glomerata
(Cocksfoot)

This long-lived, cool-season, perennial bunchgrass is grown as a meadow and pasture grass, but it sometimes gets

Orchardgrass is called cocksfoot in England for the way the bottom branch of each flower head stands out at an angle to the stem—like a thumb or a chicken's back toe.

into lawns and gardens where its coarse texture is objec-tionable. Being a bunchgrass, orchardgrass lacks spreading rhizomes and reproduces from seeds.

The Weed
Orchardgrass forms dense clumps of tufted shoots that are held together by short rhi-zomes. It is easily identified by its distinctly flattened sheath below the blade, look-ing as though it might have

been ironed. It can also be identified by its stubby, one-sided seed heads, if the weed is allowed to mature.

Control Measures
In lawns: Eliminate orchardgrass as soon as it is noticed. Cut under the root crown to remove a clump. A carefully aimed spot treatment with glyphosate (Ortho Kleenup® Grass & Weed Killer) will kill the weed. Re-seed the bare spots. If the lawn is Kentucky bluegrass, it will fill in on its own.

In gardens and around woody ornamentals: Spot-spray with glyphosate (Ortho Kleenup® Grass & Weed Killer, Ortho Kleenup® Super Edger) according to label restrictions. Orchardgrass can also be dug by hand. Clean cultivation or mulching discourages new infestations.

PARSLEY-PIERT

Alchemilla microcarpa

This tiny winter annual mea-sures only an inch or so tall and grows most commonly in bermudagrass lawns. An increasingly widespread turf weed in southern states, it commonly infests sandy soils, and branches freely close to the ground.

The Weed
The deeply cut, fan-shaped leaves are slightly downy and occur alternately on the stems. The greenish flowers, which bloom in late spring, are so inconspicuous that they are hard to find. They emerge

Despite its name parsley-piert, this pesky invader of bermudagrass lawns belongs to the same plant family as roses.

from the cone-shaped base of the upper leaves, on the op-posite side of the stem from the leaf. Parsley-piert resem-bles spurweed, another winter annual that has more deeply cut leaves and hairy stems (see page 86).

Control Measures
In lawns: When the weed is growing actively in late winter or early spring, spray with an herbicide containing 2,4-D and dicamba. A properly fertilized and managed lawn resists invasion. Where pos-sible, improve soil structure by incorporating compost or other organic matter.

PENNYWORT

Hydrocotyle umbellata
(Water pennywort, lawn pennywort, lilypads, dollarweed)

This perennial weed infests frost-free southern lawns, es-pecially those wet from rain or kept wet by excessive ir-rigation. It is a particular pest in St. Augustine grass. The round leaves contrast sharply with grass foliage. Pennywort reproduces by seeds and by stems that root at nodes, extending growth in wide patches.

Other species found inland and farther north are com-monly called pennywort (*H. sibthorpioides, H. ranunculoides, H. verticillata*). The penny-worts vary in size and detail but basically look alike, have similar growth habits, and can be similarly controlled.

The Weed
The smooth, bright green leaves are nearly round, slightly scalloped, and vary in size from that of a penny to a silver dollar. The long leaf stem, attached under the cen-ter of the blade, holds the blade aloft like a toy um-brella. Flowering stalks with crowded, nondescript blos-soms grow from the prostrate main stem during summer.

Control Measures
In lawns: Destroy patches of pennywort by applying an herbicide combining 2,4-D and MCPP (Ortho Weed-B-Gon® Lawn Weed Killer for large areas; Weed-B-Gon® Jet Weeder—Formula II for spot treatment). Use MCPP (Ortho Weed-B-Gon® for Southern Lawns) on sensitive warm-season lawns. Overwatering

Pennywort, with its shiny round leaves, is especially likely to turn up in lawns that are over-watered.

contributes to the weed prob-lem, so regulate soil moisture, and check soil fertility. Improving air circulation by pruning trees higher may also help improve turf quality.

PLANTAIN

Plantago species
(Common plantain, broadleaf plantain, Rugel's plantain, blackseed plantain, buckhorn plantain, ribgrass, narrow-leaved plantain)

Very common and unattractive, various species of plantain occur in lawns and gardens throughout the United States. White man's footprint is the name Indians used, because plantain appeared wherever early immigrants settled. The different species have leaves of different sizes, and vary in other minor ways, but they grow and are controlled similarly. Plantains grow in all kinds of soil, but prefer rich, moist sites. These ground-hugging perennial weeds suffocate desirable plants, and reproduce from seeds that germinate in spring.

The Weed

Plantain is stemless except for the tough, leafless, flowering stalks that develop during the second year and seem to defy lawn mowers. The heads of tiny greenish flowers begin appearing in spring and produce large quantities of seeds until late fall. The weed has a thick, fibrous root system and basal rosette of leaves with very prominent veins or ribs that are almost parallel and run the length of the leaf.

Reddish or purplish leaf-stalk bases distinguish blackseed (Rugel's) plantain (*P. rugelii*) from broadleaf plantain (*P. major*). Both have broadly oval leaves and long, slender flower spikes. Buckhorn (*P. lanceolata*) has longer, narrower leaves but its flower spikes, which form at the end of tall stalks, are short and compact.

Control Measures

In lawns: Before the weed forms seeds, apply 2,4-D alone or in combination with other weed killers (Ortho Weed-B-Gon® Lawn Weed Killer, Ortho Weed-B-Gon® for Southern Lawns, Ortho Crab Grass & Dandelion Killer, Ortho Chickweed & Clover Control, Ortho Chickweed, Spurge & Oxalis Killer D). Late in the season the weed may respond slowly. Leaf bases usually become puffy before treated weeds finally die. If there are only a few weeds, spot-treat with a combination of 2,4-D and MCPP (Ortho Weed-B-Gon® Jet Weeder—Formula II). Clumps can be cut out if care is taken to get well under the root crown so that no roots are left for regrowth. Good management will help develop a lawn that resists further invasion.

In gardens and around woody ornamentals: Treat with glyphosate plus oxyfluorfen (Ortho Kleenup® Super Edger) according to label restrictions. Avoid the problem of established weeds by cultivating or pulling young ones when the ground is soft. Mulching keeps new seedlings from germinating.

This broadleaf plantain shows the wide flat leaves that smother grass and defy the lawn mower.

POISON IVY

Rhus radicans, syn.
Toxicodendron radicans
(Poison creeper, three-leaved ivy, picry)
T. rydbergii
(Rydberg's poison ivy)

This plant is notorious for the severe skin rash, blisters, and inflammation that merely brushing against it can produce in most people. As with several other related, native North American plants—Pacific poison oak (*Rhus diversiloba*), and poison sumac (*Rhus vernix*—see page 78)—poison ivy leaves, stems, roots and berries contain a resin that causes an often serious allergic reaction in about 80 percent of the population. "Leaflets three, let it be" is useful advice, because all of these obnoxious plants have leaves usually composed of three distinct leaflets.

The irritating, oily resin present in all parts of poison ivy and its relatives is almost indefinitely stable. Once it contacts skin, clothing, pet fur, or tools, it is difficult to remove. Resin on tools or clothing has been known to cause a rash in highly sensitive people a year later. Lathering and rinsing three or four times with an alkaline soap within an hour of contacting the plant may prevent or minimize a reaction. The alkaline soap helps dissolve the resin, but a fat-based one spreads it further. Consult a pharmacist, dermatologist, or other physician for treatment.

Not only is poison ivy a threat to people's health, it can interfere with desirable plants too. When it grows as a vine on trees, the clinging stems can reach 75 feet in length. Poison ivy spreads by long underground roots and by seeds. New plants are often started by birds. At least

Not only does poison ivy cause most who touch it to develop an itchy rash, but it can smother trees by climbing them and blocking out the light.

55 bird species eat the fruit and distribute the seeds widely in their droppings.

Poison ivy grows along the East Coast and inland to Texas and the Midwest in woodlands, sand dunes, and fields. It can invade yards and gardens. The infestation range is continued westward and more northerly by Rydberg's poison ivy. It grows mostly in sandy woods or dry barren areas from Maryland southward and into parts of Texas, Oklahoma, and Kansas.

The Weed

Each compound poison ivy leaf usually grows at the end of a long stalk and generally has three leaflets. These are often reddish when young, changing to a glossy dark green in summer and brilliant red in fall. The pointed leaves can be of different textures and shapes on the same plant or even on the same stem. The edges of most leaves are smooth but some are toothed or occasionally lobed. Clusters of small, round, waxy, grayish white fruit appear on female plants in late summer following the small, greenish flowers. The fruit is grooved like a peeled orange, and often remains all winter. No berries form on male plants, or on poison ivy plants growing in shade.

The woody stems of poison ivy may grow as a shrub, as a slender vine running on the ground, or as a climber of trees, fences, and shrubs. When climbing it develops many aerial roots. These attach the vines securely to bark. Horizontal underground stems can extend several yards from the parent plant and send up short leafy shoots.

Rydberg's poison ivy, which requires more moisture for growth, has thicker, somewhat spoon-shaped leaflets, does not form aerial roots, and is a slow-growing shrub usually less than 3 feet tall. Its leaflets on velvety stems have rounded lobes somewhat like those of white oak. The undersides are densely covered with fine hairs, thus appearing to be lighter than the dark green upper surfaces. It spreads by rhizomes and by seeds as does poison ivy.

The vine or ground cover Virginia creeper (*Parthenocissus quinquefolia*) looks similar to poison ivy and is often confused with it. It can be distinguished from poison ivy by its five finger-shaped leaflets and blue berries. It is not allergenic.

Control Measures

Wherever found: Consider it your duty, as it is legally in some places, to destroy poison ivy plants. Spray triclopyr (Ortho Poison Ivy & Poison Oak Killer—Formula II, Ortho Brush-B-Gon® Brush Killer) on mature foliage in summer to eliminate these poisonous plants. Triclopyr will kill other broadleaf plants hit by the spray, but not grasses. If poison ivy is climbing a tree or shrub, minimize possible herbicide injury to these desirable plants by severing the climbing vines at the base and treating the stump or regrowth as directed on the label. Afterward clean the cutting tool in rubbing alcohol. Take extreme precautions against coming in contact with the foliage.

Glyphosate (Ortho Kleenup® Systemic Weed & Grass Killer) is also an effective control, especially when applied in midseason when the poison ivy is actively growing. This spray is not selective, and can kill grasses as well as broadleaf plants on contact. If the spray contacts bark of mature, thick-barked trees, no damage will be done, but it might injure young or thin-barked species.

Both herbicides are less effective if applied too early, before foliage is fully expanded. Spray again if new growth appears.

Hand-pulling or grubbing out poison ivy roots can be risky and not always effective. Any pieces of the long roots left in the ground can resprout. Wear gloves and other protection to avoid contact. Twigs or dug-up roots should be buried or bagged and discarded in the trash, *never burned*. Burning poison ivy—even seemingly old, dry debris—releases the irritant in the form of smoke particles, which can cause a severe internal reaction if inhaled.

POISON OAK

Rhus diversilobum, syn. *Toxicodendron diversilobum* (Pacific poison oak, Western poison oak)
Rhus toxicodendron, syn. *Toxicodendron toxicarium* (Poison oak)

Poison oak is similar to poison ivy in almost all of its obnoxious ways. Both contain the same resin that can cause a severe allergic rash. (See poison ivy, above.) Pacific poison oak is distributed widely west of the Sierras, north into Oregon and Washington, and in many parts of California including the seacoast and desert. It can inhabit probably the widest range of growing conditions of any of these irritating plants, even saline soils and crevices of rock piles, and is extremely tolerant of shade or intense sunlight.

The Weed

The three leaflets are irregularly lobed and variable. Some resemble the lobed leaves of certain oak species, others merely have wavy margins. Pacific poison oak sometimes looks like a vine, attaching aerial roots to an upright object, but mostly grows as an upright shrub with many small, woody stems rising from the ground. It spreads both by underground rootstocks and by seeds.

Control Measures

Wherever found: Control is the same as for poison ivy (see this page). Where Pacific poison oak has invaded cultivated areas, the choice is between determinedly grubbing it out or treating with either triclopyr (Ortho Poison Ivy & Poison Oak Killer—Formula II, Ortho Brush-B-Gon® Brush Killer) or glyphosate (Ortho Kleenup® Systemic Weed & Grass Killer, Ortho Kleenup® Grass & Weed Killer, Ortho Kleenup® Spot Weed & Grass Killer).

POISON SUMAC

Toxicodendron vernix

This plant looks quite different from its relatives poison ivy and poison oak. It is a woody shrub or small, usually leaning tree from 5 to 25 feet tall. Sap from all parts of the plant cause the same allergic reaction as poison ivy. It grows in wet areas, mostly near swamps or bogs in the

If you react to poison ivy, beware of its close relative poison sumac. Seedlings may have 3 leaflets, but the leaves of mature plants have 7 to 13 leaflets each.

eastern third of the United States except for southern Florida.

The Weed

Leaves are compound with a 2- to 4-inch long leaflet at the end and 6 to 12 more paired along a central stem. The white or green fruit of poison sumac hangs in loose clusters. New plants apparently start from seeds dropped by birds, since this weed does not form underground stems.

Shining sumac or dwarf sumac (*R. copallina*) looks similar but has wings along the leaf stem and causes no allergic reaction. Neither does staghorn sumac (*R. typhina*), which bears velvety, red fruit.

Control Measures

Control of poison sumac is the same as for poison ivy, with triclopyr or glyphosate (see this page).

Pacific poison oak is similar in appearance to and just as allergenic as poison ivy. Both plants form greenish white berries in fall.

POKEWEED

Phytolacca americana
(Pokeberry, Virginia poke, skoke, garget, pigeonberry, inkberry)

A perennial that dies to the ground in fall, pokeweed grows back again rapidly from its huge taproot the next year. It towers above most garden plants.

This weed has both good and bad aspects. Its undesirable qualities are that its roots and berries are poisonous; the purple berries stain; it reproduces readily from pro-

Pokeweed berries, dark purple when ripe, are poisonous to humans. They remain on the plant well into winter.

lific seeds spread by birds; it grows large (6 to 10 feet high); and its thick white taproot helps it survive most attempts at eradication. Its good qualities are that very young shoots can be eaten like asparagus when thoroughly cooked; the berries loose their toxicity if cooked and can be used for pies; the berries provide food for songbirds; and the root furnishes phytolacca, an important medical drug.

The Weed
Shaped almost like a small tree, pokeweed forms long branches from the big, hollow, magenta-tinged trunklike stem. The large leaves are smooth and dark green. They are mottled magenta if diseased by mosaic virus. In summer stalks of small white flowers bloom and by fall clusters of 10-seeded dark purple berries ripen.

Control Measures
In gardens and around woody ornamentals: Pokeweed is not easily controlled. Spot-treat with triclopyr in areas listed on the label. Avoid spraying nearby desirable plants by cutting down pokeweed stalks and then treating the regrowth.

Keep pokeweed cut to prevent seed formation. Try to eliminate it by pulling the taproot out entirely when the soil is moist, or cut the root well below the soil surface and chop off shoots as they appear afterward.

PRICKLY LETTUCE

Lactuca serriola, syn.
L. scariola
(Wild lettuce, milk thistle, English thistle, compass plant, Chinese lettuce, wild opium)

This unruly relative of garden lettuce occurs all over the United States except northern Maine and southern Florida. It may develop as an annual or carry over as a biennial. The weed prefers dry or light soil and is troublesome along roadways. Plants from its windblown seeds pop up in gardens too.

The Weed
Growing from a deep taproot, the upright stems are hollow, have a sticky white sap and grow 1½ to 6 feet tall. The lower part of the pale green or straw-colored stem is often prickly. The leaf base clasps the stem with arrow-shaped

Salad lettuce is a close relative of this weed, prickly lettuce. Each has milky sap, but prickly lettuce is bitter, less leafy, and has prickles.

projections; leaf edges are prickly and sharp spines line the midvein underneath, especially on the lower leaves. (Sowthistle, which it resembles, has smooth midribs with no prickles and only weak prickles on leaf margins. See page 84.) Prickly lettuce leaves are frequently turned on edge and tend to point north and south.

Yellow flower heads forming at the ends of slender branches from late spring until late fall have narrow buds. Seeds have a tuft of white hairs and float away on these parachutes if they're not broken off. In mild climates seeds germinate both in fall and spring.

Control Measures
In lawns: Apply 2,4-D (Ortho Chickweed, Spurge & Oxalis Killer D). Improve soil fertility.

In gardens and around woody ornamentals: Spot-treat with glyphosate (Ortho Kleenup® Grass & Weed Killer) according to label restrictions. Prickly lettuce is readily disposed of in vegetable gardens by cutting under the rosettes with a hoe or pulling the plants well before they flower and form seeds. Mulch to keep weeds from reappearing.

In walks, driveways, patios, etc.: Spot-treat prickly lettuce weeds with glyphosate (Ortho Kleenup® Spot Weed & Grass Killer, Ortho Kleenup® Super Edger).

PUNCTUREVINE

Tribulus terrestris
(Caltrop, ground burnut, tackweed, goathead)

This weed is armed with abundant clusters of prickly burs (nutlets). At maturity the clusters fall apart and hitch a ride on animals, rubber tires, shoe soles, or anything else their hard spines puncture. Spines are so tough they can flatten a bicycle tire. If there is enough moisture for only one of the two to four seeds in each bur to germinate, the others will stay dormant—sometimes for years—until conditions are favorable for germination.

A network of fine rootlets enables the weed to survive in spite of drought. It forms dense mats that crowd out desirable plants. A common summer annual in cultivated fields and waste places, this belligerent survivor grows from Colorado south and westward to California and in eastern and midwestern states.

The Weed
Stems are prostrate and can grow 6 to 8 feet long, branching freely from a deep taproot. The 1- to 2-inch-long leaves consist of five to eight

Puncturevine's genus name, Tribulus, *is the Latin word for a four-pronged weapon used to stop cavalry. The plant's spurred seedpod looks as if it could do just that.*

pairs of tiny leaflets covered with silken hairs. Bright yellow flowers usually open only in the morning, on cloudy days, or in shade during the summer. The vicious five-parted burs grow on the undersides of the stems.

Control Measures
In lawns: Puncturevine is controlled fairly well by 2,4-D but a combination of 2,4-D and dicamba is more effective. It is also controlled by repeated applications of methanearsonates. Following better management practices, including thickening turf and filling in bare spots, should prevent reinvasion after herbicide treatment.

In gardens and around woody ornamentals: Spot-treat with glyphosate (Ortho Kleenup® Grass & Weed Killer) according to label restrictions or chop plants off below the root crown before they flower to prevent seed formation. Mulch over cleared ground to keep new seedlings from forming.

PURSLANE

Portulaca oleracea
(Pusley, wild portulaca, pursley)

Few fertile garden soils are without this succulent-leaved, sprawling cousin of the beautiful rose moss (*P. grandiflora*). Purslane forms dense mats of stems that crowd out desirable plants. Its smooth thick leaves, stems, and roots absorb and store water, enabling it to withstand hot dry weather. Purslane infests gardens, cracks in pavement, and new or thin lawns, especially in the South.

An especially troublesome weed because of its continuous and large production of little seeds, purslane needs warm weather for germination and growth. It has a short life cycle; seedlings don't appear until soil temperatures reach 70° F to 80° F, after most other weed seedlings are destroyed by cultivation. Seeds mature within two weeks after flowers open and can germinate a week later.

Eaten as a vegetable in many parts of the world, purslane is also a formidable pest because of the huge number of seeds it produces.

The Weed
Stems are succulent and often purplish red. Coming from a taproot, they branch freely and often form mats with broad, thick stemless leaves whose margins are smooth and tips rounded. The pale yellow flowers are stemless too and bloom from early summer until frost, although the individual flowers open only for about four hours on a single sunny morning. (In hot regions it blooms from mid- to late spring and dies; more purslane germinates in late summer and flowers until frost.) The thick fleshy primary root has many fibrous secondary roots that do not go especially deep but can quickly absorb water during and after rain.

Among look-alikes, prostrate pigweed (*Amaranthus blitoides*) has a tougher stem and thin leaves (see page 81). Spotted spurge (*Euphorbia maculata*) has thinner stems and leaves and milky juice (see page 86).

Control Measures
In lawns: A preemergent herbicide applied for crabgrass control, such as DCPA (Dacthal®—Ortho Garden Weed Preventer), will have dissipated by the time purslane germinates; it can be reapplied in early summer. Where purslane appears in turf, kill it with a combination of 2,4-D and MCPP (Ortho Weed-B-Gon® Lawn Weed Killer for large areas; Ortho Weed-B-Gon® Weed Killer for spot treatment) or with a combination of MCPP and dicamba (Ortho Chickweed, Spurge & Oxalis Killer D). Then take steps to grow thicker turf. Use MCPP (Ortho Weed-B-Gon® for Southern Lawns) on warm-season grasses.

In gardens and around woody ornamentals: Early control is critical. Apply DCPA (Dacthal®—Ortho Garden Weed Preventer) or trifluralin shortly before high temperatures and weed germination are expected. Germination can also be prevented with a 4- to 6-inch layer of mulch.

To kill emerged weeds, spot-treat with glyphosate (Ortho Kleenup® Grass & Weed Killer). It is easy to kill purslane in the seedling stage with frequent shallow cultivation. Burn or compost uprooted plants to prevent continued seed ripening or rerooting. Plants are able to reroot after being inactive for several weeks.

QUACKGRASS

Agropyron repens
(Couchgrass, witchgrass, twichgrass, quitchgrass, skutchgrass, wheatgrass, Shellygrass, knotgrass, devilsgrass)

This aggressive and strongly competitive perennial grass came to the United States, probably as a grain contaminant, long before the American Revolution. Its extensive creeping, light-colored rhizomes (underground stems) grow vigorously in cool fall and early spring weather and may increase in length by 5 feet a year. Their sharp tips are as hard as ivory and able to pierce any plants in their way. Fibrous roots form at each scaly node along the rhizome and new stalks can grow from there. A single node, grown without competition, produced 14 rhizomes totalling 458 feet in one year. Quackgrass roots emit two toxic substances that help the plant in its competition with desirable plants. Seeds are most likely to germinate in spring from the upper ½ to 1 inch of soil. About a quarter of the seeds germinate the first year after being formed but some are known to have stayed alive after being buried 14 years.

When reproduced from rhizomes all the plants are similar. There is a great deal of genetic variation—including response to herbicides—when plants grow from seeds.

Most common in northern states, quackgrass occurs in all

Look for clasping auricles (little ear-shaped appendages at the base of leaf blades) to help identify quackgrass, one of the most tenacious of grassy weeds.

except the most southern states. It invades lawns, other landscaped areas, and unmaintained areas.

The Weed
Stalks reach 1 to 3 feet tall. From spring to early fall wheatlike flower stalks bloom and produce seeds. The weed can be identified by flat leaves with distinct auricles (tiny ears) like hooks that clasp the stem at the base of the blade. Perennial ryegrass also has

auricles but they are short and don't clasp the stem. The leaves of perennial ryegrass are very glossy underneath.

Control Measures
In lawns: Because of the extensive network of rhizomes, there is no effective selective control. For severe infestations kill the lawn with glyphosate and reseed. Frequent close mowing reduces nutrient reserves and eventually kills quackgrass. Follow good management practices to encourage vigorous turf.

In gardens and around woody ornamentals: Careful control with herbicides is most practical. Fluazifop-butyl (Ortho Grass-B-Gon® Grass Killer) can be used selectively for controlling quackgrass growing with listed ornamentals. Careful spot treatment with glyphosate (Ortho Kleenup® Grass & Weed Killer) controls quackgrass in flower gardens.

Digging up and exposing roots to the drying action of the hot summer sun aids in control but any pieces left behind will sprout. Frequent cultivation before new shoots are more than an inch tall eventually exhausts nutrient reserves, weakening and finally killing the quackgrass. Leave cultivated soil rough (do not smooth out surface) over the winter to expose and kill quackgrass roots. Small patches can be eliminated by keeping them covered with black plastic or roofing paper for at least a year.

RAGWEED, COMMON

Ambrosia artemisiifolia
(Wild tansy, hogweed, bitterweed, hayfever weed, blackweed)

One of the most common garden weeds—along with crabgrass, purslane, and pigweed—ragweed fills the air

Because common ragweed seedlings die when heavily shaded, a thick healthy lawn or a well-mulched vegetable garden effectively prevents infestations.

for miles around in late summer and fall with huge quantities of very light pollen that makes 3 to 5 percent of the population miserable with hayfever. (Goldenrod is accused of doing this because its showy blooms appear at the same time as ragweed's unremarkable ones; however, goldenrod's pollen grains are too heavy and waxy to even float in the air, much less cause hayfever.)

By late spring most of the seeds have germinated. Only a few more seedlings emerge during the summer. They do not develop if they are heavily shaded at emergence. Ragweed can invade lawns, vegetable gardens, and other landscaped areas.

The Weed
An annual, common ragweed grows 1 to 6 feet tall and has a taproot and sturdy, shallow lateral roots. The 2- to 4-inch-long leaves are fernlike. The plant bears both male and female flowers. As the day length shortens in summer, hundreds of small, greenish male flowers form in spikes—even after being repeatedly mowed along roadsides—and continue blooming until plants are killed by frost. Seeds are produced by stalkless female flowers snuggled down at the leaf bases.

Giant ragweed (*A. trifida*) is an annual that can grow 10 to 20 feet tall. It has quite different leaves—large, slightly hairy, and most with three distinctly pointed lobes. Western ragweed (*A. psilostachya*),

whose rough leaves more closely resemble those of common ragweed, is generally a perennial that reproduces by creeping roots and rhizomes (underground stems) as well as by seeds. Pollen from these species causes just as much distress as that of common ragweed.

Control Measures
In lawns: Ragweed may appear in new lawns. It is also a symptom of poor turf growth in established lawns. It can easily be discouraged by fertilizing and mowing so that a tight cover shades the soil where ragweed seeds might otherwise germinate. Use bromoxynil to kill seedling ragweed in newly seeded lawns or 2,4-D (Ortho Weed-B-Gon® Lawn Weed Killer) when the grass has become established.

In gardens: Cultivate or hand-pull weeds early in the season. Mulching is highly effective in vegetable and flower gardens. Ragweed is less of a problem with late planted vegetables than with early ones like carrot, corn, and potato.

Around woody ornamentals: Spot-treat with glyphosate (Ortho Kleenup® Systemic Weed & Grass Killer). Existing ragweed can be hand-pulled or hoed. Maintain a permanent mulch to prevent weed germination.

REDROOT PIGWEED

Amaranthus retroflexus
(Rough pigweed, carelessweed, Chinamans greens)

Of the many annual pigweeds, redroot is one of the most common and troublesome in gardens and cultivated fields. Young plants begin flowering when only a few inches tall. Myriads of tiny seeds are liberated throughout the growing season, providing countless seedlings in following years. The seeds ripen in a vessel whose cap comes off like the lid of a sugar bowl.

The weed prefers hot dry spots and is a pest in vacant lots, roadsides, lawns, and gardens.

The Weed
Redroot pigweed usually grows upright but forms mats in mowed lawns. The roots are reddish or pink and the stems are usually reddish near the base. The dull green leaves are roughly diamond-shaped, somewhat hairy, and prominently veined. Flowers are either female or male; they have no petals and are surrounded by scales or bracts that give them a rough, strawlike texture.

Prostrate pigweed (*A. blitoides*) has axillary flowers on very short branches and forms thick mats although it does not root at the nodes. Tumble pigweed (*A. albus*) is a western species that is moving east. Its flowers are crowded in small clusters in leaf axils of whitish stems. As tumble pigweed matures its leaves fall off, the stems bend inward, and it breaks from the ground and rolls or is blown away, scattering seeds as it goes. Smooth pigweed (*A. hybridus*) is similar to redroot pigweed but not as hairy and it has somewhat finer flowers and shorter flower clusters.

Control Measures
In lawns: Use 2,4-D (Ortho Weed-B-Gon® Lawn Weed

Redroot pigweed looks like a plainer version of its colorful relative the domestic amaranth.

Killer) when pigweed is actively growing. Use MCPP (Ortho Weed-B-Gon® for Southern Lawns) on warm-season grasses.

In gardens and around woody ornamentals: Prevent the weed with DCPA (Dacthal®—Ortho Garden Weed Preventer) in areas listed on the label. Spot-treat emerged weeds with glyphosate (Ortho Kleenup® Grass & Weed Killer). Hand-pulling also works well. Pull or hoe seedlings as soon as they are seen to prevent flowering and seed set. A thick mulch will keep weeds from reappearing.

RED SORREL

Rumex acetosella
(Sheep sorrel, field sorrel, horse sorrel, cow sorrel, mountain sorrel, toad sorrel, gentleman's sorrel, sourgrass, redweed)

Because its leaves taste like vinegar, red sorrel is sometimes called sourgrass. Although often considered an indicator of acid soil, red sorrel also thrives in neutral or slightly alkaline soils, especially if they are low in nitrate nitrogen. Stems grow low, several coming from the root crown to invade new areas. Red sorrel thrives in cool moist weather but is a pest even in dry sandy soil in lawns and landscaped areas. It can grow as an annual but far more commonly is a perennial with a rather woody and extensive, although shallow, root system.

The Weed
A small spreading plant growing 4 to 14 inches tall, red sorrel has stems that form loose clumps. Leaves are shaped like arrowheads; they are narrow and thin at first, becoming broad and succulent by late summer. Flowers appear from spring to fall. The slender upright flower stalks contain either yellowish male or reddish female flowers clustered in whorls. Curly dock (*Rumex crispus*) is one of many red sorrel relatives known collectively as dock. Dock has lance-shaped leaves and flower stalks that are up to 3 feet tall. (For photographs of curly dock, see page 12.)

Control Measures
In lawns: Only a minor weed in turf, red sorrel can be controlled with an herbicide combining 2,4-D and MCPP (Ortho Weed-B-Gon® Lawn Weed Killer) or 2,4-D and

Red sorrel plants are very small, although flowering stems may reach a foot tall if they aren't in a mowed lawn.

dicamba (Ortho Chickweed, Spurge & Oxalis Killer D). Repeat the application if regrowth appears. Spot-treat

with a combination of 2,4-D and MCPP (Ortho Weed-B-Gon® Weed Killer). Apply adequate fertilizer, especially nitrogen, and lime. Determine the proper amount and proportion by having the soil analyzed.

In gardens: Grub out the shallow rootstocks and add them to the compost heap. Add nitrogen, lime (except around acid-loving plants), or other fertilizer elements as indicated by soil analysis. Mulching keeps runners close to the surface where they can be readily removed.

Around woody ornamentals: Prevent red sorrel with dichlobenil applied in late fall or winter. Destroy the roots by shallow cultivation, removing every bit to avoid starting new colonies. A permanent mulch, preferably a fabric type, will keep the area weed-free. Glyphosate (Ortho Kleenup® Super Edger) can be used if applied carefully to avoid touching thin-barked trunks or branches, but cultural control is usually adequate.

REDSTEM FILAREE

Erodium cicutarium
(Alfilaria, pinclover, pingrass, storksbill, heronsbill, filaree)

A western member of the geranium family, redstem filaree is also abundant in the East. It is a troublesome cool-season annual or sometimes a biennial. Although filarees are pretty plants, their prolific seeding capability brands them as weeds. The spindle-shaped, ¼-inch-long seeds have an amazing flail-like hairy tail an inch or more long that is twisted tightly like a corkscrew when dry. When wet it uncurls and can drive the pinkish tan seed into the soil. Seeds germinate in fall or under cool, moist conditions.

The Weed
Redstem filaree forms mats of erect, spreading, or prostrate

It's fun to watch the tails of redstem filaree seedpods twist, but sobering to know that the twisting pushes the seeds into the soil.

stems 3 to 12 inches long. It has finely divided leaflets in pairs along the leafstalk. Early stalkless basal leaves grow in a rosette; as it matures it branches and may grow to 2 feet tall or stay low on the ground, covering a couple of feet or more. Umbrellalike clusters of five-petaled rose or purplish flowers produce seed pods that are unusually long and needlelike, hence the name storksbill. Leaflet lobing is not as fine or deep in broadleaf filaree (*E. botrys*), a leafier, more relaxed annual with seed pod beaks 3 to 5 inches long. Those of white-stem filaree (*E. moschatum*) are only about ½ inch long. This plant is somewhat larger than either of the other filarees and its stems are fleshy and whitish to light green.

Control Measures
In lawns: Apply a combination of 2,4-D and MCPP (Ortho Weed-B-Gon® for large areas, Ortho Weed-B-Gon® Jet Weeder—Formula II for spot treatment) in early spring or in fall in warm-winter climates soon after germination to prevent spread. Thicken turf by improving soil conditions with proper fertilization and watering.

In gardens: In established plantings use a hoe to remove rosettes below the root crown, then clean cultivate or mulch so seedlings don't reappear. In vegetable gardens cultivate shallowly before planting to get as many weed seedlings as possible to germinate, then remove these by cultivating through the growing season or apply mulch. A preemergent application of trifluralin in areas listed on the label will minimize seedling emergence.

Around woody ornamentals: Apply the preemergent dichlobenil. Control emerged plants as in gardens or spray with glyphosate (Ortho Kleenup® Weed & Grass Killer).

RUSSIAN THISTLE

Salsola iberica, syn. *S. kali* var. *tenuifolia*
(Tumbling weed, Russian tumbleweed, windwitch, saltwort, prickly glasswort)

A thoroughly disagreeable, extremely spiny annual plant, Russian thistle becomes hard and woody with maturity. It breaks loose at the ground to form tumbling balls that each spread 20,000 to 50,000 seeds as they roll along. Russian thistle is a favorite host of

Tumbling along with the tumbleweed, also called Russian thistle, are tumbleweed seeds that are spreading the weed into areas far from the wild West.

sugar beet leafhoppers, which carry the virus causing blight of spinach, tomato, bean, and other plants.

The weed occurs mostly in dry western regions and eastern and southern coastal states but is rapidly spreading into other areas. Russian thistle came to South Dakota as an impurity in flax seeds, and within only 20 years had spread to 16 states and all the Canadian provinces.

The Weed
The many stems are smooth, often reddish and tender when young but become rigid as the weed matures. Early leaves drop off and are replaced by shorter, stiff awl-shaped ones that end in spines. Small green flowers with no petals are borne in axils (angle formed by leaf and stem) from near the bottom to the tip of the plant starting in midsummer.

Control Measures
In lawns: Russian thistle can be controlled by any of the phenoxy herbicides such as 2,4-D, 2,4-DP (dichlorprop) and MCPP (Ortho Weed-B-Gon® Lawn Weed Killer), especially if combined with dicamba (Ortho Chickweed, Spurge & Oxalis Killer D). Improve soil conditions.

In gardens: Practice clean cultivation, hoeing off any stray weeds. Germination can be prevented by a preemergent application of benefin or trifluralin in areas listed on the label. Maintaining a thick mulch is the most

sensible control method. Clean out fence corners and cut off scattered plants, then burn them to keep seeds from spreading.

Around woody ornamentals: Glyphosate (Ortho Kleenup® Super Edger) can be used to kill existing plants. A hoe is equally effective. Mulching is the best way to keep weeds from reestablishing.

SALSIFY, COMMON

Tragopogon porrifolius
(Goatsbeard, oysterplant, vegetable oyster)

This weed is among the many plants related to and resembling dandelions. Although not a serious pest it is widespread in the United States, having been introduced from Europe for its large, fleshy edible taproot. It reportedly tastes somewhat like oysters when cooked.

The Weed
Common salsify is a biennial or perennial. Its blue-green leaves are long, narrow, and smooth-edged and taper to

Meadow salsify (top) has yellow flowers, but its large attractive seed heads closely resemble those of the purple-flowered common salsify.

the tip from a clasping base. Stems grow 2 to 4 feet tall, branching from the base if allowed to mature. Purple flowers similar to those of dandelions usually do not appear until early in the plant's second summer. Each seed has a brownish upright cup of feathery bristles that waft it wherever the wind blows.

Meadow salsify (*T. pratensis*) has yellow flowers and somewhat broader leaves. Western salsify (*T. dubius*), also called meadow salsify or goatsbeard, grows 2 to nearly 3 feet tall and has lemon yellow flowers that follow the sun. Its flower stalks are hollow and the elegant gauzelike seed bristles glisten white.

Flower arrangers preserve them intact with hairspray. All have milky juice and are biennials or perennials that usually have only leaves the first year, followed by flowers the second year.

Control Measures
In gardens: Grow salsify as a vegetable or destroy it ruthlessly the first year by hoeing or pulling. Close the door to new seedlings by maintaining a mulch.

SANDBUR

Cenchrus incertus, syn.
C. pauciflorus
(Field sandbur, burgrass, sandspur)
C. longispinus
(Longspine sandbur)

Whoever steps on a sandbur—with or without shoes—doesn't have to be told what it is. Troublesome in sandy lawns and gardens mainly because of its hard, spiny burs, this native American grass invades lawns, orchards, gardens, and unmaintained areas, especially where soil is sandy. Roots are fibrous, sometimes forming on the nodes where the spreading branches touch soil. The weed often spreads by the burs hitching rides on clothing and animal fur.

Field sandbur occurs across the southern third of the United States from coast to coast and longspine sandbur has spread to all states except Washington, Idaho, and Montana. Sandburs are usually annuals but may overwinter as short-lived perennials.

The Weed
The tufted plants of field sandbur grow 6 inches to 2 feet tall; leaves are smooth, narrow, yellow-green, and borne on stems that are flat as though ironed. Plants may grow upright or form mats if mowed. Flowers appear from mid-summer to autumn, then develop burs containing 8 to 40 spines.

Sandbur, an annual grass, has wicked spurs on its seeds. They have caused many an injury to unguarded feet or hands.

Control Measures

In lawns: Sandbur is a grass and hence not killed by broadleaf herbicides. Prevent the weed by applying benefin or trifluralin.

Methanearsonate (Ortho Crabgrass & Nutgrass Killer) can be used to kill sandbur in most major lawn grasses except St. Augustine grass, carpetgrass, and centipedegrass. Some turf may be temporarily discolored by the treatment, which must be repeated within a week for satisfactory control. Improve fertilization and general management to thicken turf.

In gardens and around woody ornamentals: Benefin and trifluralin can be applied around certain ornamental and vegetable plants as a pre-emergent; check the label. Spot-treat with fluazifop-butyl (Ortho Grass-B-Gon® Grass Killer). Young plants, which have a reddish base, are easily removed by shallow cultivation since the root system is weak. Mulching discourages the reappearance of the weed.

SHEPHERDS-PURSE

Capsella bursa-pastoris
(Ladyspurse, pepperplant, caseweed, pickpurse)

Into nearly every garden comes this most common of weeds. Belonging to the mustard family, shepherdspurse is named for its flat valentine-shaped seedpods filled with innumerable small seeds that are scattered by the wind. Seeds are long-lived, lying dormant in the soil until conditions are favorable for germination.

The Weed

Starting as a rosette of usually hairy and variously lobed leaves, the weed sends up a single leafless stalk with small white flowers. These are followed by seedpods containing

Heart-shaped seedpods identify shepherdspurse, an annual weed best controlled by preventing seed formation.

shiny orange-brown seeds. Shepherdspurse is an annual, germinating in fall and living through the winter or germinating in early spring.

Control Measures

In lawns: Treat weeds with 2,4-D (Ortho Weed-B-Gon® Lawn Weed Killer). Improve fertilization and general management of the lawn.

In gardens: Keep weed populations low by cultivating early in spring, occasionally as the season advances, and again thoroughly in fall. The weed is easily kept out by mulching.

SOUTHERN BRASSBUTTONS

Cotula australis
(Australian brassbuttons)

An annual weed, southern brassbuttons has round, flattened flower heads that look like brass buttons. Leaves of this low-growing weed have a strong scent. Although not very troublesome in gardens, southern brassbuttons is a serious pest in lawns. Common brassbuttons (*C. coronopifolia*) is more widespread geographically, but less of a problem even though it is perennial.

The Weed

The leaves are covered by soft hairs and deeply divided so it closely resembles spurweed (see page 86). Buttonlike flowers are borne above the foliage on slender stems 1 to 2 inches long, whereas spurweed flowers are daisylike and have no stem. When young, southern brassbuttons may also be mistaken for pineappleweed (*Matricaria matricarioides*), which has a nice fruity fragrance and cone-shaped flower heads, or for mayweed (*Anthemis cotula*), which has rank-smelling, finger leaves and flower heads with white petals (see page 71).

Control Measures

In lawns: Aerate to relieve compaction if that is a problem. Not affected by 2,4-D alone, brassbuttons responds to formulations that also contain dicamba. Keep the lawn thick to resist further invasion.

In gardens: Remove by hand and mulch to prevent a reappearance of the weeds.

Around woody ornamentals: Apply glyphosate (Ortho Kleenup® Systemic Weed & Grass Killer) to kill existing weeds. Stop a reoccurrence with a permanent mulch.

SOWTHISTLE

Sonchus oleraceus
(Hares lettuce, colewort, milkthistle, annual sowthistle)
S. asper
(Prickly sowthistle, spiny sowthistle)

Of the group of prickly weeds called thistles, sowthistle is the best known and most widely spread. Found throughout the United States, it is most common in the South and along the West Coast in rich soil in gardens and occasionally in lawns and other landscapes.

The Weed

Sowthistle is an upright plant with a taproot. The leaves are lobed almost to the midrib and have earlike projections that clasp the stem. The stem oozes a milky sap when broken. The clustered heads of yellow flowers bloom all summer. Hares lettuce and prickly sowthistle look alike but the latter has very spiny leaves.

Finely divided leaves and small flower heads on wiry stems characterize southern brassbuttons.

Prickly sowthistle, one of the most common lawn and garden weeds in the United States, is a taprooted annual.

Control Measures

In lawns: Sowthistle is easily killed by 2,4-D (Ortho Weed-B-Gon® Lawn Weed Killer). Keep it out by improving turf so that it resists invasion. Liming the soil if it is acid may also help.

In gardens: Conquer sowthistle with clean cultivation and by hoeing or hand-pulling (wear gloves) plants before they flower. If the weeds are blooming get them to the compost heap quickly because seeds may mature even after plants have been uprooted.

Around woody ornamentals: Mulching prevents invasion. Apply a combination of glyphosate and oxyfluorfen (Ortho Kleenup® Super Edger) to kill existing weeds and prevent emergence of more weeds for up to three months.

SPEEDWELL

Veronica species
(Veronica)

Although delightful to look at in spring when its delicate flowers bloom, speedwell is objectionable in lawns and gardens because it is an overly energetic creeper. The many species of this common weed are generally referred to simply as speedwell or veronica.

Two—perennial slender speedwell (*V. filiformis*) and winter annual corn speedwell (*V. arvensis*)—are very aggressive and, therefore, more serious pests than the others.

Three—common speedwell, (*V. officinalis*), slender speedwell, and thymeleaf speedwell (*V. serpyllifolia*)—are distinctly perennial, living for many years and rooting where their stems creep on or under the ground. Three more—field speedwell (*V. agrestis*), purslane speedwell (*V. peregrina*), and birdseye or Persian speedwell (*V. persica*)—are annuals, growing through the summer and then dying. Like corn speedwell, ivyleaf speedwell (*V. hederifolia*) is a winter annual that grows during the cooler parts of the year and disappears when weather turns hot.

The Weed

Most species of speedwell have small, rounded, and slightly toothed leaves. Their dainty flowers have four lobes and may be clear blue, lilac blue, or white and are followed by fat heart-shaped seed capsules. They have fibrous roots.

Two—perennial thymeleaf and annual purslane speedwell—can be identified by their smooth leaves. The others are hairy. Four—annual purslane, corn, and field speedwells and perennial thymeleaf speedwell—can be recognized by mostly single or very few upright stems. The rest branch freely and spread on the ground.

Slender speedwell is a perennial that spreads great carpets of sky blue flowers in northern lawns at the same time that dandelions bloom. Growing in sun or shade, it can invade even the healthiest lawn but doesn't usually smother it. The weed does not produce fertile seed but makes up for that by starting new colonies wherever bits of the creeping stems are dropped. It is also spread by lawn mowers.

One way speedwells are spread is on lawn mowers. The slender stems catch in the machine, then drop in another part of the lawn where they take root.

Corn speedwell invades thin lawns in the South, its green leaves contrasting with brown dormant warm-season grass. Corn speedwell flowers are tiny sparks of blue, have no stem, and are borne tightly all along the upper two thirds of the plant. Birdseye or Persian speedwell looks much the same but has longer stems that usually lie on the ground and its flowers are on slender stalks. Field speedwell, another look-alike, is smaller.

Control Measures

In lawns: Speedwells do not respond well to most selective herbicides. A combination of 2,4-D and MCPP or 2,4-D and dicamba (Ortho Weed-B-Gon® Lawn Weed Killer, Ortho Chickweed, Spurge & Oxalis Killer D) reduces corn speedwell. Repeat the treatment if some still survives. Thickening the lawn will make it more resistant to weed invasion. A wettable powder, not granular, formulation of DCPA (Dacthal®) applied in late fall or early spring slowly affects slender speedwell so it disappears by the following spring.

In gardens: Clean cultivation, especially early in the year when the winter annual speedwells are growing actively, followed by a thick mulch is the primary way of controlling the weeds.

Around woody ornamentals: Keep the weeds out with a thick mulch. Treat existing speedwells with a combination of glyphosate and oxyfluorfen (Ortho Kleenup® Super Edger).

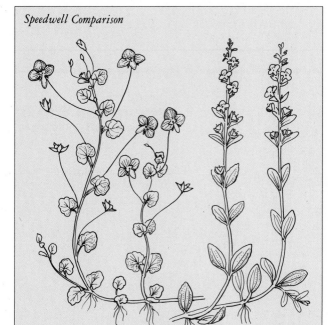

Speedwell Comparison

The pretty blue-flowered speedwells are easy to confuse. Slender speedwell (left) has hairy, rounded leaves and its flowers bloom on long stalks. Thymeleaf speedwell (right) has smooth, oblong leaves, and its flowers bloom on short stalks near the stem. Both are aggressive perennials.

SPOTTED SPURGE

Euphorbia maculata, syn.
E. supina
(Milk purslane, spotted
pursley, prostrate spotted
spurge, milk spurge)

The weed forms flat mats in
lawns and gardens and in
cracks in walks and drives,
spreading widely and branching and rebranching. The
branches, however, never
root. Spotted spurge tolerates
very close mowing and flourishes during hot, dry weather
that throws cool-season
grasses into semidormancy.
An annual, its seedlings
sprout in spring beginning
when the soil temperature
reaches 55° F to 60° F. Several thousand seeds can be
produced from each plant in a
single season; these germinate
at different times. This prolific weed, a true hot weather
annual, becomes very aggressive by midsummer.

Plant and leaf size vary
depending on growing con-
ditions—small in crevices between flagstones or other
paving and two to three times
as large in well-nourished
lawns or gardens.

The Weed
The little, smooth oval leaves,
which vary from dark green to
red, generally have a reddish
brown blotch on the upper
surface and are opposite on
the stem. Stems are low-growing, fanning out from the taproot. Clusters of tiny pinkish
white flowers form in leaf
axils (angle formed by leaf
and stem) all season until the

plant is killed by frost. As
with poinsettia and many
other relatives, all spurge parts
have milky sap.

There are many other simi-
lar-appearing spurges, but
most respond to the same
control methods. Creeping
spurge (*Chamaesyce serpens*) is
becoming a problem because
it can root from nodes and no
selective control has been
found. It has smaller, more
rounded leaves and shorter
intervals between leaves than
prostrate spurge.

Control Measures
In lawns: Apply a pre-
emergent treatment of DCPA
(Dacthal®) in early spring before germination and again
eight weeks later. On emerged
weeds apply a combination of
2,4-D and MCPP (Ortho
Weed-B-Gon® Lawn Weed
Killer) or 2,4-D and dicamba
(Ortho Chickweed, Spurge &
Oxalis Killer D) while the
spurge is still young and before cool-season lawn grasses
are under stress from drought
or high temperatures. Reapply
a week later if spurge continues to grow. Since more seeds
germinate throughout the
summer, the treatment must
be repeated. Improve any
weak aspect of management
to assure a thick lawn.

In gardens: Clean-cultivate
early before weeds start to
flower or form seed. It is easy
to grasp a mat of stems and
pull out the short root.

Around woody
ornamentals: Prevent seedlings by applying dichlobenil
(Ortho Casoron® Granules) or

by keeping the area well
mulched.

In walks, driveways, patios,
etc.: Use glyphosate (Ortho
Kleenup® Systemic Weed &
Grass Killer) where no vegetation is desired. Prometon
(Ortho Triox® Vegetation
Killer) can be used to control
spotted spurge if there are no
tree or shrub roots in the area.

SPURWEED

Soliva sessilis
(Burweed, carpet burweed,
lawn burweed, soliva)

Primarily a pest in the South,
this low-growing winter
annual resembles southern
brassbuttons (see page 84)
with a very sharp difference—
it has a hardened skin-piercing

*The spur in spurweed refers to a
very real sharp spine that makes
this weed an unpleasant lawn
invader.*

spike at the tip of each seed.
Seedlings emerge from open
ground in early fall and mature the following spring. A
heavy population can literally
carpet the ground. When hot
weather arrives the plants die
out leaving behind plenty of
seeds to germinate when
weather is again cool.

The Weed
Plants grow 2 to 6 inches
wide. The leaves are deeply
cut, very finely hairy, and
stalked. Flower heads are
stemless and without petals.
One to three of them occur
at the base of each leaf.

Control Measures
In lawns: Preemergent herbicides are not effective, but
existing weeds can be controlled with MCPP (Ortho
Weed-B-Gon® for Southern
Lawns) or bromoxynil.

In gardens: Keep soil clean
with cultivation, especially in
late fall and early spring. Then
apply mulch.

Around woody
ornamentals: Avoid invasion
by mulching. Dichlobenil or
a combination of glyphosate
and oxyfluorfen (Ortho
Kleenup® Super Edger) can
be used if spurweed is a
problem.

STINGING NETTLE

Urtica dioica
(Tall nettle, slender nettle,
seven-minute itch)

This harmless-looking weed
has powerful weapons—bristles on the leaves and stems
that are actually tiny, brittle,
glassy tubes. When brushed
against they break off and in-
ject a substance that causes an
intense burning sensation that
can be relieved by washing
with dilute rubbing alcohol.
Growing mostly on rich soil
in neglected places, the weed
also sneaks into shrub plantings. Stinging nettle re-
produces by seeds and
creeping rootstocks.

The Weed
The stems of this perennial
grow 3 to 6 feet tall, have
four ridges, and are stout but
hollow. Pairs of leaves along
the stem are rather thin,
approximately egg- or heart-
shaped, and sharply toothed.
The weed blooms in late summer. Small greenish male
flowers form on short spikes
near the top of the plant and
female flowers hang in strings
from the axils (angle formed
by leaf and stem) of lower
leaves. Both kinds of flowers
usually appear on the same
plant. Seeds mature from early
fall until frost kills the plant
to the ground.

*Spotted spurge is one of the flattest weeds, often escaping a mower's
blades by being so low to the ground.*

Although the pain it causes usually lasts less than a day, stinging nettle can make you very sorry you brushed against its foliage, which bears irritating hairs.

Control Measures

Wherever found: Mow close, cutting the tops off in June and again in August and burning or composting them to prevent seeds. Roots grubbed out will die if allowed to dry. Around woody ornamentals use glyphosate (Ortho Kleenup® Super Edger) to control stinging nettle.

TOADFLAX

Linaria vulgaris
(Butter-and-eggs, yellow toadflax, Ranstead weed, wild snapdragon, impudent lawyer)

Spikes of the snapdragonlike flowers of toadflax commonly cover many eastern and Pacific coast roadsides but the weed can be found in

Related to snapdragon, toadflax can be quite ill-mannered when it grows where it isn't wanted. It is resistant to most herbicides.

all states. Colonies spread aggressively with extensive creeping perennial roots, making it a difficult weed to control.

The Weed

Plants are upright, grow 6 inches to 3 feet tall, and have narrow pale green leaves. The two-toned yellow flowers have a tail and inflated lips that can be pressed open between thumb and finger. An orange spot appears on each lower lip. The flowers have an unpleasant odor and bloom from summer through fall, forming seeds as late as November.

Control Measures

In lawns: Apply MCPP (Ortho Weed-B-Gon® for Southern Lawns for large areas, Ortho Weed-B-Gon® Weed Killer for spot treatment).

In gardens: Constant cultivation and removal of roots will eventually exhaust nutrient reserves and end the infestation. Toadflax is resistant to most herbicides but can be controlled with glyphosate (Ortho Kleenup® Systemic Weed & Grass Killer) if the infestation is serious.

TRUMPET-CREEPER

Campsis radicans
(Cow-itch)

Where cold climates limit its growth, trumpetcreeper is a handsome ornamental vine with flaring orange or scarlet tubular flowers and dark green leaves. In mild climates it becomes an obnoxious weed wherever it gets loose.

It is native throughout the eastern half of the United States except the northern areas and grows in Iowa and across much of Texas. Trumpetcreeper's winged seeds whirl to new locations where they root deeply. If plants are cut off at ground level, pieces of the vigorous running roots left behind send up fresh shoots. Even the part removed may form new roots and start growing again.

The Weed

A woody perennial vine with stems 15 to 40 feet long, trumpetcreeper hoists itself by aerial rootlets to heights of 75 feet. Each of its large leaves is composed of 7 to 11 leaflets with notched edges. Showy

A colorful climber, trumpetcreeper can become a rampant weed where winters are mild.

flowers begin to open in early summer with seeds forming soon afterward. Its 4- to 6-inch-long pods are filled with winged seeds.

Control Measures

Wherever found: Sever vines and treat the cut stubs with triclopyr (Ortho Brush-B-Gon® Brush Killer).

VELVETGRASS

Holcus lanatus
(Mesquitegrass, German velvetgrass)

When mature velvetgrass is covered with soft gray velvety hairs that make it stand out in a green lawn. It grows best in moist, rich soil and is, therefore, especially troublesome in the Pacific Northwest. Flowers appear early in spring, releasing seeds by midsummer. The whole flower clusters fall away then leaving bare stalks.

The Weed

This upright perennial grass has slender rhizomes (underground stems) that form small patches. Leaves are 4 to 8 inches long. Plants reach 2 to 4 feet tall if unmowed or they flatten into a rosette of gray stems where mowed. Flowers have a purplish tinge.

Control Measures

In lawns: Keep the weed mowed to prevent seed formation. With no selective control available, the choice is between cutting the weed below the root crown or spot-treating with glyphosate. If the clump was small, surrounding lawn grass will probably heal over. Otherwise, reseed or sod bare spots.

In gardens and around woody ornamentals: Spot-treat with a combination of glyphosate and oxyfluorfen (Ortho Kleenup® Super Edger). Hand-pull, dig or cultivate to eliminate weeds. Mulch to prevent new weeds.

Velvetgrass thrives under the same conditions as cool-season lawn grasses, but its pale color mars the look of a perfect lawn.

VELVETLEAF

Abutilon theophrasti
(Butterprint, Indian mallow, pieprint, cottonweed, American jute, Indian hemp)

This husky, fast-growing annual makes the most of its short life. It's able to grow almost anywhere and compete with the strongest cultivated plants. Velvetleaf seeds are known to have survived in soil for 50 years, so it becomes a continual pest once it appears in a lawn or garden. A hot-weather plant, its seeds may not germinate until mid-July but it grows quickly after that. Winter winds shake thousands of seeds from the seedpods blowing them long distances.

The Weed
Velvetleaf is deep rooted. Where there is room it branches and may reach 6 feet tall. Even when very small the plant is easily identified by its broad, velvety, heart-shaped leaves. Yellow five-petaled flowers form singly in leaf axils (angle formed by leaf and stem). Their many stamens are united into a column characteristic of related plants like hollyhock and hibiscus. The ornamental 1-inch-wide seed vessels are much larger than the flowers and contain little bean-shaped seeds.

Control Measures
In lawns: Use 2,4-D combined with MCPP and dicamba (Ortho Chickweed, Spurge & Oxalis D Killer).

In gardens: Cultivate intensively to destroy seedlings and prevent flowering and seed set. Once seeds have spread the weed becomes a long-term problem.

VENUSLOOKING-GLASS

Triodanis perfoliata, syn. *Specularia perfoliata*
(Clasping bellwort)

Although its flowers are attractive, this small wandlike member of the bluebell family is an almost irrepressible weed, seeding widely in open, sterile soils. The earliest flowers are low on the stem, have no petals, and never open. These fertilize themselves and produce many seeds that ripen and are sown before the showier flowers farther up the stems bloom.

The Weed
This upright annual, growing 8 to 24 inches tall, has clasping heart-shaped leaves. The pretty flowers with five violet-blue petals bloom along the upper part of the stems and continue seed formation after the inconspicuous lower flowers have matured.

Control Measures
In gardens: Uproot or cut off this weed early, before the hidden flowers form seeds in late spring. Continue to pull or cultivate lightly through the summer. Enrich the soil by fertilizing and adding organic matter.

By the time the violet-blue upper flowers of Venuslookingglass are visible, the lower inconspicuous flowers have already seeded the garden.

VIOLET

Viola species
(Common blue violet, wild pansy, field pansy, johnny-jump-up)

Generations of children have delighted in picking the white-centered flower whose name describes its color.

The common blue violet may be considered either a wildflower or a weed, depending on whether it is competing with other plants in a garden or spoiling the lawn.

However, violets are considered weeds when their broad, shiny, slightly scalloped heart-shaped leaves mar the perfection of a velvety lawn or grow in gardens where other plants are preferred. They spread by branching rootstocks that grow thicker each year and seed themselves prolifically.

Some of the seeds are produced the usual way but more come from inconspicuous flowers at the base of the plant. These fertilize themselves without ever opening, have no petals, and are so fat that they are sometimes mistaken for bulbs. Breaking one open will reveal a large number of brownish seeds that can greatly increase the violet population.

The violet family is a huge one with several dozen species and varieties. Those that most frequently annoy home gardeners by growing in lawns and cultivated areas are the perennial common blue violet (*V. papilionacea*); annual wild pansy or field violet (*V. arvensis*), which sometimes lives for a second year; and little field pansy or johnny-jump-up (*V. rafinesquii*, syn. *V. kitaibelliana*), a winter annual that disappears during hot weather.

The Weed
Wild pansies have slender spreading stems and what appear to be tufts of leaves at each node. They have miniature pale yellow or white and yellow flowers on long stalks from late spring to mid-summer and occasionally in autumn.

Field pansy or johnny-jump-up spreads widely in turf early in the spring, its tiny blossoms looking like fragile white or bluish porcelain. The leaves are spoon-shaped but have large stipules (appendages at the base) that look like deeply cut divisions.

Control Measures
In lawns: Close mowing is ineffective because of the hidden flowers. Thicken turf to resist the annual species. Chemical control is efficient,

Velvetleaf seeds are long-lived—they have been known to germinate after being buried in soil for over 50 years.

although not always perfect. Ester formulations of 2,4-DP (dichlorprop) combined with 2,4-D work best. Late summer or early fall, when turf and weeds are both growing actively is the most favorable time for treatment. A second treatment a week later increases control.

In gardens and around woody ornamentals: Use DCPA (Dacthal®—Ortho Garden Weed Preventer) in listed cases to prevent seedling emergence of all but field pansy or johnny-jump-up. Hand-pull existing weeds, prying out any thick roots to ensure complete removal, or treat with a combination of glyphosate and oxyfluorfen (Ortho Kleenup® Super Edger) around woody ornamentals.

VIRGINIA BUTTONWEED

Diodia virginiana

Until recently Virginia buttonweed occurred mostly in the wild—growing in ditches, marshes, and other wet places—but it is becoming more widespread and invading cultivated areas. It is an increasingly serious problem in turf, where it makes dense mats. Very close mowing merely encourages it to grow closer to the ground. Initially seen as a strong competitor in warm-season grasses, patches of the weed are appearing in cool-season lawns in dry areas too.

A relatively recent invader of home gardens, Virginia buttonweed forms dense perennial mats in lawns.

The Weed
Virginia buttonweed is a perennial with fleshy roots and a woody root crown. Tough, slightly fuzzy branching stems spread rapidly, root at nodes, and make dense, coarse-looking mats. The smooth dark-green leaves are an inch or more long, slenderly elliptical, and opposite each other along the stems. Delicate white hairs cover the inner surface of small white flowers that appear singly in leaf axils (angle formed by leaf and stem). Poorjoe (*Diodia teres*) looks much the same but its flowers lack hairs. It is an annual and is not as serious a competitor.

Control Measures
In lawns: There is not yet a good control labeled for this new problem weed. Keep runners raked so they can be cut off, minimizing spread. Destroy all clippings to prevent their rooting in new places. Monthly applications of 2,4-D combined with dicamba or with dichlorprop (2,4-DP) have been more effective than 2,4-D alone or any other combination in preventing regrowth for four to six weeks.

In gardens: Dig out the weed wherever seen and destroy it.

Around woody ornamentals: Prevent infestations with dichlobenil or spot-treat with glyphosate.

VIRGINIA PEPPERWEED

Lepidium virginicum
(Field peppergrass, birdseed, poormans pepper, tonguegrass, birds pepper)

The most common of several species of peppergrass, Virginia pepperweed is the most troublesome one in lawns but can and does grow almost anywhere else. It starts in fall or early spring as a small rosette of smooth, irregularly

Stems of notched round seedpods identify Virginia pepperweed as the problem. Get it out before the seeds ripen.

cut leaves that may be mistaken for shepherdspurse (see page 84). No matter—they're both annual mustards and behave alike. Virginia pepperweed can also grow as a winter annual or a biennial depending on the climate.

The Weed
Arising from a simple taproot, the weed has upright branched stems ending in flowering stalks. The upper leaves have a tapering base and somewhat toothed margins. Blossoms with four small white or greenish petals form seeds over a long period. Many flat, round seedpods along the stems look like tiny notched paddles and have a pungent peppery taste. The upper leaves of field peppergrass (*L. campestre*) clasp the stem with an arrow-shaped leaf base. The lower leaves are gray-green and covered with soft hairs.

Control Measures
In lawns: Like other members of the large mustard family, Virginia pepperweed is easily controlled with 2,4-D. Thicken the turf by fertilizing and proper mowing to discourage reinvasion.

In gardens and around woody ornamentals: Remove rosettes by cultivating lightly in early spring. Hand-pull any that are near desirable plants. Keep all flowers and seed heads cut. Peppergrass seeds can germinate the same year they ripen. Mulch to conserve moisture, improve soil texture, and remove seedlings right away.

WILD BLACKBERRY AND BRAMBLES

Rubus species
(Blackberry, dewberry, raspberry, thimbleberry)

Wonderful when their fruits can be enjoyed, wild blackberry and related brambles are dreadful when they form great thorny thickets fit only for sheltering rabbits. These semiwoody perennial shrubs spread by shoots sent up from their roots as well as by seeds spread by birds.

Some western species are evergreen, holding their foliage over great mounds in open areas or along roadsides. Himalaya blackberry (*Rubus discolor*) is one of these and its seedlings may pop up almost anywhere, even from beneath stone mulch.

The Weed
There are over 300 bramble species with stems that are trailing, upright, or arching and that often root at the tips. They follow the same pattern of growth as cultivated ones do, developing canes in two stages. For example, the first-year canes of Allegheny blackberry (*R. allegheniensis*) are ridged and covered with downy hairs and have scattered thorns and compound leaves mostly with five leaflets. During the second year leaves on those canes have only three leaflets. Canes grow upright bearing pyramids of small, white, five-petaled flowers that produce fruit

Turn your back on wild blackberry and it will start to dig in, rooting from arching stems and sprouting from buds on the roots.

and then die. The prickly dead stems remain in place and add to the general jumble as new canes emerge.

Control Measures

Around woody ornamentals: If the brambles have invaded plantings of woody ornamentals, cut the stems and immediately apply undiluted triclopyr (Ortho Brush-B-Gon® Brush Killer, Ortho Poison Ivy & Poison Oak Killer—Formula II) on the stubs. Nonselective glyphosate (Ortho Kleenup® Systemic Weed & Grass Killer) can be applied to the foliage thoroughly, but take great care to avoid spraying desirable plants. Early fall, when canes are still growing actively but before a killing frost, is the best time for herbicide treatment.

WILD CARROT

Daucus carota
(Queen Anne's lace, birdsnest plant, crowsnest, devils plague)

This biennial (occasionally annual or perennial, depending on growing conditions) wildflower of fields and roadsides was introduced to North America from Europe. It is a Eurasian relative of the cultivated carrot but is not edible. Its prolific seeds are sticky and get carried far and wide on clothing and on animals. As a weed it invades gardens and lawns. The rosettes look harmless enough the first summer but grow

tall, flower, and set seed the second summer. Wild carrot manages to flower even after it has been mowed short.

The Weed

Rosettes of ferny leaves form the first year. The second year the woody white taproot grows deeper, and from late spring or early summer until fall, bristly hollow stalks raise lacy parasols of tiny white or pinkish flowers with a single dark maroon flower in the center. As seeds begin to develop after the little petals fall, the head pulls together upward forming the brown bird's nest that gives the plant one of its common names. The seeds have several rows of spines that stick to clothing or animal fur. An oil in the seeds and other plant parts smells like carrots.

Control Measures

In lawns: Wild carrot is easily controlled by a postemergent application of 2,4-D (Ortho Weed-B-Gon® Lawn Weed

Its flowers are attractive in a meadow or a florist's bouquet, but wild carrot is an invasive weed in gardens. Eliminate it the first year before it can bloom and seed itself.

Killer for large areas, Ortho Weed B-Gon® Weed Killer for spot treatment). It seldom persists after that if the lawn is kept thick.

In gardens: Destroy tender seedlings by ruthless cultivation or hand-pull when the soil is moist. With frequent cultivation more and more seeds can be induced to germinate and then be destroyed. Mulch to avoid further germination.

WILD GARLIC

Allium vineale
(Field garlic, scallion, wild onion, crow garlic)

A perennial weed, wild garlic reproduces in three ways. Bulbs, bulblets, and seeds all keep wild garlic in lawns and gardens where its waving tops are unattractive, especially when growing through a dormant warm-season lawn.

The Weed

A cool-season plant, wild garlic grows in clumps from bulbs that survive cold and

drought. Its leaves are hollow and round, while those of wild onion (*A. canadense*) are solid and flat.

There are two types of wild garlic plants. A very common type develops only leaves that grow from the base of a large central bulb with one or two hard-shelled bulbs pressed tightly against it. If not kept cut the other type of wild garlic produces a head with many aerial bulblets at the end of a tall leafless stem. Its greenish or purplish flowers produce seeds in all but northern areas. This type has one large soft bulb underground and one to six smaller hard-shelled bulbs, each of which can form a new plant.

About 25 percent of the hard-shelled bulbs sprout the year after they form. The rest may not start active growth for as long as five years. Active bulbs and seeds start sprouting in late summer and continue through fall. When temperatures are warm, these plants grow through winter to spring. The underground bulbs form in very early

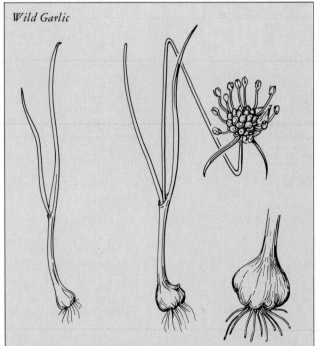

Wild Garlic

One type of wild garlic (left) produces large bulbs underground. The other type (center) also produces aerial bulbs in the flower head at the tip of a leafless stem. At the end of the season, the underground bulbs (right) somewhat resemble garlic.

A serious pest in lawns, wild garlic permeates the air with a pungent smell when mowed.

spring and emerged leaves die back by late spring. New leaves appear the next fall.

Control Measures

In lawns: In fall, spray 2,4-D (Ortho Weed-B-Gon® Lawn Weed Killer for large areas; Ortho Weed-B-Gon® Weed Killer, Ortho Weed-B-Gon® Jet Weeder—Formula II for spot treatment) on clumps. Repeat the treatment early the next spring to control new shoots. The next fall treat tops coming from the remaining hard-shelled bulbs. Otherwise the cycle of bulb formation and infestation will continue.

In gardens: Casual pulling merely increases wild garlic by breaking off bulblets, which will continue to grow. Dig clumps out, being careful to remove all the underground bulbs and bulblets. Even a single one left behind will produce a new plant. Check the soil surface after rain or irrigation and remove any exposed bulblets, because they have a special kind of root (retractile) that will pull them back into the ground.

Around woody ornamentals: Remove clumps by hand or apply glyphosate (Ortho Kleenup® Super Edger) in spring when the maximum number of bulbs and bulblets have formed tops to absorb the herbicide. Repeat the treatment to control any additional wild garlic tops that may emerge.

WOODSORREL

Oxalis species
(Oxalis, sourgrass, wood shamrock)

Often difficult to distinguish from each other, woodsorrel comprises a group of similar plants that hybridize and form variants. Control is not always easy and learning to tell them apart is sometimes necessary when deciding how to effectively eradicate these troublesome weeds.

Their main survival technique involves a unique manner of seed dispersal. As seed capsules mature during the summer, the internal pressure increases until an elastic jacket bursts and throws the seeds as far as 6 feet away. The seeds can germinate and start new plants quickly, although there is variation in the time and range of conditions under which they can germinate.

Perennial creeping woodsorrel (*O. corniculata*) is a serious problem in plantings or containers of woody ornamentals, in gardens, and in lawns where its habit of rooting at each node on long slender runners makes it extremely hard to remove by hand. It is about as difficult to eliminate chemically because it is resistant to most selective herbicides.

The Weed

All woodsorrels have cloverlike leaves whose three leaflets are heart-shaped, smooth, and thin and have a distinctive sour taste from the oxalic acid they contain. The leaves are generally green but forms with reddish foliage often occur, especially in creeping woodsorrel. Most species have shallow fibrous roots. Some have rose or violet flowers, but the species that are annoying in lawns and gardens produce small, yellow, five-petaled flowers all summer. The explosive cucumber-shaped seedpods soon follow.

Rocket-shaped seedpods of woodsorrel shoot seeds as far away as 6 feet. Ample seeds combine with rooting stems or perennial bulbs to make this a formidable garden pest.

Yellow woodsorrel (*O. stricta*) becomes especially conspicuous in cool-season lawns by midsummer when heat and drought have reduced active growth of grasses. It may grow as an annual or a short-lived perennial and sometimes sends up several shoots from its roots.

The upright annual European woodsorrel (*O. europaea*) often appears in gardens.

One other distinctive oxalis dots lawns and gardens in California—perennial Bermuda buttercup (*O. pes-caprae*). A tall stemless escapee from gardens, it displays large, bright yellow flowers in early spring. It grows from a deep rootstock with small bulbs, making it extremely difficult to control. Its tops disappear after blooming.

Control Measures

In lawns: Yellow woodsorrel can be controlled readily with an herbicide containing dicamba (Ortho Chickweed, Spurge & Oxalis Killer D) or MCPP (Ortho Weed-B-Gon® Lawn Weed Killer, Ortho Weed-B-Gon® for Southern Lawns for large areas; Ortho Weed-B-Gon® Jet Weeder—Formula II for spot treatment). Creeping woodsorrel is resistant to all herbicides except triclopyr, which can only be applied by a licensed professional.

In gardens: Hand-pull newly formed tops of woodsorrel before flowers appear. Because of its persistent rooting habits, creeping woodsorrel is much harder to eliminate, but it can be done if all parts are consistently

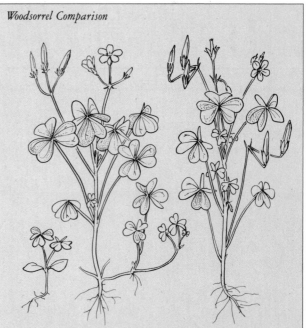

Woodsorrel Comparison

Learning to distinguish woodsorrel species can help in their control. Perennial creeping woodsorrel (left), which is difficult to control, bears flowers on upreaching stalks. Yellow woodsorrel, (right), which is easily controlled by herbicides, has blossoms appearing on stalks that form right angles to the stem.

grubbed out and new shoots removed as soon as they appear. Continue shallow cultivation to catch any new seedlings or missed pieces. Spot-treat with glyphosate (Ortho Kleenup® Grass & Weed Killer) in flower beds.

Around woody ornamentals: A woven type of fabric mulch topped with ground bark or a similar material discourages most woodsorrel plants. Especially sturdy ones may poke through. In that case glyphosate (Ortho Kleenup® Systemic Weed & Grass Killer, Ortho Kleenup® Super Edger) is the best way to get rid of them.

YARROW

Achillea millefolium
(Milfoil, fernweed, bloodwort, thousand-leaf)

This is an obstinate perennial weed whose tough rhizomes (underground stems) make it a problem in gardens and lawns, where it forms feathery patches when mowed. Its presence in lawns often indicates infertile, acid soil, although yarrow can grow under a wide range of conditions.

The Weed
The lance-shaped leaves are usually covered with fine hairs and are finely divided so that their appearance is delicate and fernlike. The foliage has

It's a good idea to get a soil test if yarrow invades the lawn. Yarrow can take over a lawn if soil is infertile and acid.

a strong odor and tastes bitter. If flower stems are allowed to form, they can grow 1 to 2 feet tall. At the top they bear stiffly branched, dense, flat-topped clusters of very small white or pinkish flowers in early summer. Yarrow is able to reproduce from its creeping rhizomes or by flat, oblong seeds that ripen from late summer onward.

Control Measures
In lawns: Yarrow responds well to 2,4-D combined with dicamba or with MCPP (Ortho Weed-B-Gon® Lawn Weed Killer, Ortho Chickweed, Spurge & Oxalis Killer D) but not to 2,4-D alone. Chemical control must be coupled with cultural improvements to thicken the lawn so that it can compete better and avoid reinfestation. It is advisable to have the soil analyzed for best guidance in soil improvement.

In gardens: The rhizomes grow close to the surface and can be grubbed out without difficulty. Check soil fertility and pH to see if either needs correction and add compost or other organic material as necessary.

Around woody ornamentals: Grub out all rhizomes or destroy them chemically with glyphosate (Ortho Kleenup® Super Edger), repeating the treatment if control from the initial treatment is not complete. Fertilize adequately.

YELLOW ROCKET

Barbarea vulgaris
(Herb barbara, bittercress, wintercress, yellow-weed)

Members of the large mustard family have remarkably similar white flowers, but yellow rocket stands out from the group because it covers cultivated fields with a dramatic display of golden flowers in early spring. A biennial or

The flowers of yellow rocket are cheering in the spring, but don't let seeds form or the weed will be an increasing problem for several years.

short-lived perennial, it reproduces mainly by seeds. It has a taproot but sometimes spreads by new shoots developing from crowns of old roots.

The Weed
Young plants overwinter as rosettes of shiny, dark green, coarsely lobed leaves during the first year. Flowering stems from the root crown have progressively shorter leaves that are less lobed, especially on the flower stalks themselves. Wild mustard (*Sinapis arvensis*) blooms later and has lighter yellow flowers and hairy stems. Seeds of both plants form in slender pods. Wild radish (*Raphanus raphanistrum*) is also similar but it is an annual, has stiffly hairy leaves and stems, and blooms much later. Curious constrictions make the seedpod resemble upright strings of beads.

Control Measures
In lawns: In new lawns control seedlings with a prompt application of bromoxynil or 2,4-D after the grass has become established well enough to have been mowed twice.

In gardens: Cut rosettes from their roots the first year so they won't flower or form seeds. Although seeds live in the soil for several years, shallow cultivation can reduce and finally eliminate these weedy mustards. Mulching is an effective deterrent, too.

YELLOW STARTHISTLE

Centaurea solstitialis
(St. Barnaby's thistle)

Colonies of this bristly weed dot the United States. It is most common in the West, especially coastal California. In lawns the long, rigid yellow spines jutting out from the yellow flower heads can be very painful to bare feet.

The Weed
Yellow starthistle grows 1 to 3 feet tall if unmowed. The leaves and stems are covered with cottony hairs that make them look gray, like those of blue-flowered cornflower or

Yellow starthistle adapts to mowed lawns by forming horizontal flower stems. Its spines are a painful surprise for people walking barefoot on the lawn.

bachelor's button (*Centaurea cyanus*), a close ornamental relative. Rosette leaves are deeply cut and 2 to 3 inches long; those along the flower stem are narrow, shorter, and sharp-pointed. Unlike Russian knapweed (*C. repens*), another relative, yellow starthistle is an annual, has a simple taproot, and reproduces solely by seeds. It blooms from midspring until frost.

Control Measures
In lawns: Spray with 2,4-D (Ortho Weed-B-Gon® Lawn Weed Killer) before the weed flowers. Wet the foliage thoroughly. Take steps to thicken the turf.

In gardens: Hoe the tops off. Mulching may help keep more weeds from appearing.

INDEX

U.S. MEASURE AND METRIC MEASURE CONVERSION CHART

	Symbol	Formulas for Exact Measures When you know:	Multiply by:	To find:	Rounded Measures for Quick Reference		
Mass (Weight)	oz	ounces	28.35	grams	1 oz		= 30 g
	lb	pounds	0.45	kilograms	4 oz		= 115 g
	g	grams	0.035	ounces	8 oz		= 225 g
	kg	kilograms	2.2	pounds	16 oz	= 1 lb	= 450 g
					32 oz	= 2 lb	= 900 g
					36 oz	= 2¼ lb	= 1,000g (1 kg)
Volume	tsp	teaspoons	5.0	milliliters	¼ tsp	= 1/24 oz	= 1 ml
	tbsp	tablespoons	15.0	milliliters	½ tsp	= 1/12 oz	= 2 ml
	fl oz	fluid ounces	29.57	milliliters	1 tsp	= 1/6 oz	= 5 ml
	c	cups	0.24	liters	1 tbsp	= ½ oz	= 15 ml
	pt	pints	0.47	liters	1 c	= 8 oz	= 250 ml
	qt	quarts	0.95	liters	2 c (1 pt)	= 16 oz	= 500 ml
	gal	gallons	3.785	liters	4 c (1 qt)	= 32 oz	= 1 liter
	ml	milliliters	0.034	fluid ounces	4 qt (1 gal)	= 128 oz	= 3¾ liter
Length	in.	inches	2.54	centimeters	⅜ in.	= 1 cm	
	ft	feet	30.48	centimeters	1 in.	= 2.5 cm	
	yd	yards	0.9144	meters	2 in.	= 5 cm	
	mi	miles	1.609	kilometers	2½ in.	= 6.5 cm	
	km	kilometers	0.621	miles	12 in. (1 ft)	= 30 cm	
	m	meters	1.094	yards	1 yd	= 90 cm	
	cm	centimeters	0.39	inches	100 ft	= 30 m	
					1 mi	= 1.6 km	
Temperature	°F	Fahrenheit	5/9 (after subtracting 32)	Celsius	32°F	= 0°C	
					68°F	= 20°C	
	°C	Celsius	9/5 (then add 32)	Fahrenheit	212°F	= 100°C	
Area	$in.^2$	square inches	6.452	square centimeters	1 $in.^2$	= 6.5 cm^2	
	ft^2	square feet	929.0	square centimeters	1 ft^2	= 930 cm^2	
	yd^2	square yards	8361.0	square centimeters	1 yd^2	= 8360 cm^2	
	a.	acres	0.4047	hectares	1 a.	= 4050 m^2	

Proof-of-Purchase
0-89721-197-9